MICHAEL JACKSON

TREASURES

MICHAEL JACKSON
TREASURES

CELEBRATING THE KING OF POP
in MEMORABILIA *and* PHOTOS

JASON KING

SIMON & SCHUSTER

LONDON NEW YORK SYDNEY TORONTO

First published in Great Britain by Simon & Schuster UK Ltd., 2009

A CBS Company

1 3 5 7 9 10 8 6 4 2

Simon & Schuster UK, Ltd.

1st Floor

222 Gray's Inn Road

London WC1X 8HB

www.simonandschuster.co.uk

Simon & Schuster Australia

Sydney

A CIP catalogue record for this book is available from the British Library.

ISBN: 978-1-84737-797-5

Printed and bound in China through Legend Color Ltd Hong Kong

CONTENTS

PROLOGUE: A KING DIES

A MODEST ONE-STORY BUNGALOW WITH WHITE SIDING AND BROWN BRICK

exterior stands at 2300 Jackson Street, on the corner of West 23rd Avenue in the impoverished, dilapidated midtown of Gary, Indiana. The street got its name from the nineteenth-century American president—not, as you might think, from the pop superstar who spent his formative years there. The house at 2300 Jackson has two windows for eyes, a brick chimney for a hat, and a black iron screen door, meant to repel unwanted visitors, for a mouth.

On a summery afternoon, a week after Michael Jackson's untimely death from cardiac arrest on June 25, 2009, vivid yellow police tape cordons off 2300 Jackson's exterior. Stuffed animals, charred seven-day-old candles, and well-wishers' handcrafted collages form a three-foot-deep moat. Jackson mourners have gathered on the front lawn, wandering around like shell-shocked zombies. A white-haired woman hums in a soulful wobble. A young girl holding a Michael Jackson poster weeps deep chest sobs, pressed against her mother's bosom. Two teenagers in baseball caps give wide-eyed interviews to a television reporter. Off in the distance a car radio comes into focus blasting

---

above MICHAEL JACKSON PERFORMS AT A 1988 CONCERT IN LOS ANGELES, CALIFORNIA.
previous JACKSON CULTIVATED A STREET-SMART IMAGE AFTER THE RELEASE OF HIS 1987 ALBUM, *BAD*.

THROUGHOUT THE LATE 1970S, MICHAEL JACKSON
WORKED TO ESTABLISH HIMSELF AS A SOLO ARTIST.

MICHAEL JACKSON IN THE VIDEO FOR "BILLIE JEAN."
THE SONG WON HIM TWO GRAMMY AWARDS IN 1984, FOR
BEST R&B SONG AND BEST R&B VOCAL PERFORMANCE.

the 1983 Jackson classic "P.Y.T. (Pretty Young Thing)" As quickly as it arrives, the sound floats away again.

In death, Michael seemed just as fleeting—his incandescent flame extinguished before its time. And yet, at fifty, Michael Jackson was no flash-in-the-pan star: he had been performing professionally for nearly forty-five years. A supremely gifted and singular talent, Jackson transformed pop music, dance, and video, raising the bar for artistic excellence in each area simultaneously. Jackson sang and shouted and spun and moonwalked in fierce, joyous exultation; few entertainers in any style or genre ever matched his energetic flair. At his death, he held the record for the biggest-selling album of all time, 1982's *Thriller*, and he co-wrote the massively influential 1985 charity anthem "We Are the World." By the mid-'80s, Michael Jackson was the world's richest entertainer and the most recognizable person on earth. A hero to many for his efforts in mainstreaming black culture and for his humanitarian efforts, Jackson elicited nearly cultlike devotion from worldwide legions of fans.

Jackson's rags-to-riches story confirmed that the American dream—the potential for anyone to achieve great success—is not just a myth. But it has also forced us to confront the nightmare that often lurks on the other side of spectacular success. Jackson was a polarizing figure. Some gravitated to his trademark eccentricity; others saw unchecked narcissism. A formerly cherubic child star, Jackson matured into a tabloid fixture. He began to transform in front of our eyes as a parade of furtive

cosmetic surgeries and concealed illnesses somehow made him look racially indeterminate and androgynous. Then in the early '90s, Jackson's peculiarities took a darker turn when he came under investigation for child molestation charges. Some perceive him as a villain, manipulating the media to his own ends; others see him as an innocent, misunderstood Peter Pan, ridiculed by the mass media. There seems to be no shade of gray.

Near the end, Jackson had been acquitted of his most recent charges and was living abroad with his three children. His album sales had dropped off, and he hadn't released a new project in eight years. Huge legal fees and ill-advised business decisions—compounded by years of prescription drug addiction—left Jackson

above NOVEMBER 8, 1979, AT NASSAU COLISEUM IN UNIONDALE, NEW YORK.

facing imminent bankruptcy. Jackson was at his lowest point, in need of career rejuvenation and cash.

In March 2009, Jackson announced his comeback with This Is It, a multi-million-dollar concert residency produced by AEG Live at London's O2 arena scheduled to start that July. The resulting hysteria was palpable: the staggered run of fifty shows sold out in mere hours. Jackson seemed immediately relevant once again. However, he may not have been in the requisite physical condition to carry off those concerts. The day before his demise he was in rehearsal at Los Angeles's Staples Center: he looked gaunt, but gleaming. At 1:30 PM Pacific time on June 25, the news broke that Jackson had suffered cardiac arrest at his rented Holmby Hills residence. Rumors quickly surfaced that the culprits were

his longtime drug addiction and use of anesthesia to battle chronic insomnia. Shocked fans formed spontaneous vigils on street corners from Harlem, New York to Lima, Peru. For many, that outpouring jolted memories of the ways Michael had impacted our lives.

I grew up in suburban western Canada at the tail end of the disco craze. For my sixth birthday, my mother gave me two records: Kool and the Gang's *Celebrate* and *Michael Jackson: Superstar,* a Motown Records tenth anniversary compilation of Jackson's greatest solo hits. Those were the first vinyl albums I ever owned. Bopping to songs like "Rockin' Robin" and "Ben," I became fascinated by the earnest-looking boy with the bushy Afro on the black-and-white dust jacket. I began to trail Jackson, watching every move he made in his career,

above WHEN HE DIED, AT AGE FIFTY, JACKSON HAD BEEN PERFORMING FOR OVER FOUR DECADES. *opposite* JACKSON DOES A HIGH-FLYING JUMP IN HIS PERFORMANCE AT THE DEMOCRATIC NATIONAL COMMITTEE BENEFIT CONCERT, HELD AT NEW YORK'S APOLLO THEATER IN APRIL 2002. THROUGHOUT HIS CAREER, JACKSON PERFORMED FOR, AND RECEIVED COMMENDATIONS FROM, BOTH DEMOCRATIC AND REPUBLICAN PRESIDENTS.

obsessed with the details and nuances of his stardom. Like many young boys of the era, I didn't just want to be like him—I wanted to *be* him. I doused my hair in pomade and water so that I could have his Jheri curl. I wore one glove, pants that were hopelessly short, and white socks. I was glued to the television set that delirious evening he dazzled the world on the *Motown 25: Yesterday, Today, Forever* special.

Years later, I'd evolved into both an admirer and a skeptic. One of the first essays on popular culture that I published discussed the cultural impact of Jackson's video *Scream*. In 2004, I gave a speech at a Yale conference that centered on his impact on race and gender.

Jackson deliberately blurred the line between the real and the unreal, the authentic and the inauthentic. He puzzled us while he was alive and he continues to puzzle us in death. Perhaps that's why people all over the world responded so viscerally to the news of his passing. For those hundreds upon hundreds of millions of us who danced and sang and laughed and cried to his music and videos, we'd almost forgotten how Michael Jackson had become such an integral part of our lives— for better or worse. Whether you worshiped or despised him, Jackson is so deeply embedded in our culture that his death demands your attention in the same way that his art and his life continually compel you to look.

The book you now read isn't a comprehensive take on Jackson's life. Nor is it an investigative exposé. It's a subjective retelling of how Michael Jackson made that heroic leap from local hopeful to global superstar, touching upon the highs and lows that shaped him along the way. As we begin to unravel Jackson's complexities in the pages that follow, we're also somehow unraveling our own.

opposite AS JACKSON'S PHYSICAL APPEARANCE CHANGED, CRITICISM AND GOSSIP SWIRLED AROUND HIM. *above* JACKSON PERFORMS IN MUMBAI, INDIA, IN 1996, AS PART OF THE HISTORY TOUR.

CHAPTER ONE

A LOT
OF KNOW

"I DID NOT BELIEVE THAT SOMEONE THAT YOUNG COULD
HAVE THAT MUCH FEELING AND SOUL AND KNOW. HE HAD
A LOT OF KNOW. HE HAD—HE HAD TO KNOW SOMETHING
TO SING THAT SONG LIKE THAT."

– Smokey Robinson, Michael Jackson's memorial service, July 7, 2009

G ary, Indiana, is thirty miles east of Chicago on the south shore of Lake
Michigan. But before it was a town, Gary was a concept. The United
States Steel Corporation created Gary around a state-of-the-art steel mill
complex that promised financial opportunities to settlers. At the turn of the twentieth
century, Gary hyped itself as "the city of the century." But by the 1960s, after years
of black and Latino migration followed by white flight, Gary had descended into a
morass of urban decay.

Michael Jackson, born August 29, 1958, was the seventh of nine children: baby
brother to Maureen, Jackie, Tito, Jermaine, LaToya, and Marlon, and older brother
to Randy and Janet. Their father, Joe, a crane operator at the steel mill, played guitar
in local cover band, the Falcons, but stashed his six-string dreams in the closet to
support his growing family. His wife, Katherine, steely but mild, supplemented the

opposite EVEN AS A PRE-TEEN, JACKSON HAD A PRETERNATURAL ABILITY
TO MIMIC THE PERFORMANCES OF ICONIC STARS LIKE JAMES BROWN
AND JOHNNY MATHIS. "I'M STILL AMAZED AT HOW MY VOICE USED TO
SOUND," HE ONCE SAID. "THEY USED TO TELL ME I HAD THE VOICE OF A
THIRTY-FIVE-YEAR-OLD WHEN IT CAME TO PHRASING AND CONTROL."

family income with a part-time gig at Sears. Conservative family values pervaded the Jackson household. Joe was a lapsed Lutheran; Katherine raised her children as Jehovah's Witnesses. In keeping with Witness doctrine, the family avoided "pagan" customs: they did not celebrate birthdays or holidays. Michael and his sister LaToya visited Kingdom Hall three times a week and evangelized door-to-door.

Music infused the Jackson household. Country-and-western fan Katherine led her children in harmonized versions of Southern hymns and folk songs like "Wabash Cannonball" and "Oh! Susanna." Michael added '60s R&B and classic Rodgers & Hammerstein show tunes to his growing musical diet. Nearby

Roosevelt High School boasted a big band that sometimes marched down Jackson Street: vibrant horns and booming percussion became emblazoned into Michael's memory.

When he was around ten or eleven, Tito retrieved Joe's dusty Falcons guitar from the closet and began to practice. In time, Jackie (on vocals and shaker) and Jermaine (on bass) followed suit. Joe was infuriated—he had strictly forbidden the children from messing with his pricey instrument. But he also recognized budding talent. Joe told biographer Nelson George: "When I saw that they liked it, I kept them at it, I helped them when it got hard for them and when they felt disgusted as kids sometimes do." Katherine guided the trio, as well, and

above AN EXTERIOR PHOTO OF MICHAEL JACKSON'S MODEST, ONE-STORY BOYHOOD HOME AT 2300 JACKSON STREET IN GARY, INDIANA. THIS PHOTO WAS TAKEN IN JUNE 2003, WHEN MICHAEL RETURNED TO GARY TO VISIT HIS OLD HAUNTS FOR THE FIRST TIME IN NEARLY THIRTY YEARS. THIS WAS ALSO HIS LAST TRIP HOME.

KATHERINE ESTHER SCRUSE JACKSON, THE
MATRIARCH OF THE JACKSON FAMILY, PICTURED IN
1974 IN HER KITCHEN AT THE FAMILY'S HAYVENHURST
COMPOUND IN ENCINO, CALIFORNIA.

the boys became skilled enough to perform at local talent shows. Three soon became four when Marlon, age six, joined on bongos and vocals.

STARTING EARLY

In 1964, fresh-faced Michael wowed his first-grade class with a throaty rendition of *The Sound of Music*'s "Climb Every Mountain." He was a clever imitator. Brother Jackie recalled, in Nelson George's 1984 biography *The Michael Jackson Story,* how Michael "would see somebody do something and he could do it right away." Michael told *Right On!* magazine he developed his sensitive approach from crooner Johnny Mathis. "Before I began to develop my own style . . . I wanted to sound just like Johnny. I had never heard such a smooth voice before." As a student at Garnett Elementary, Michael dazzled classmates at lunch-hour sock hops with nimble footwork cribbed from James Brown.

Michael soon supplanted Jermaine as lead singer. Now a quintet, their work ethic was formidable. The

above THE JACKSON 5 IN AN EARLY, PRE-MOTOWN PUBLICITY STILL, LIKELY TAKEN AROUND 1966. MICHAEL IS ON THE FAR RIGHT. THE SIXTH MEMBER IS JOHNNY PORTER JACKSON, A DRUMMER HIRED TO FILL OUT THE GROUP'S SOUND—HE IS NOT RELATED TO THE FAMILY.

Jackson 5, as they'd come to be known, practiced before school, after school, and all weekend. It paid off: the boys racked up prizes at every talent competition, including a talent show at Roosevelt High where they sang the Tempations's "My Girl." The boys graduated to paying gigs, making their debut at local dive Mr. Lucky's Lounge on Grant and 11th. They made seven dollars. "The house was loaded with trophies," Michael told *Creem* magazine years later. "We always had money and we could always buy things the other kids couldn't, like extra candy and extra bubblegum."

The Jackson 5 had developed a solid amateur reputation in Gary, and they'd also ventured into neighboring Chicago in hopes of making a splash. Now, they began to perform on the "chitlin' circuit," the gritty stretch of black performing venues strewed along the northeast and southern United States. "If you didn't learn survival while working the Apollo in New York, the Regal in Chicago, the Howard in Washington, DC, and the Uptown in Philadelphia," Michael reminisced to *Jet* magazine, "you never would."

The Jacksons fell into a grueling schedule, sometimes being pulled from bed to do shows at three in the morning, that wouldn't be legally sanctioned today for child performers. Michael reflected to writer Paul Theroux years later, "I was seven or eight. Some of these were clubs or private parties at people's houses. We'd have to perform."

The Jackson 5 garnered a massive buzz along the circuit. *Soul Train* founder Don Cornelius recalled

to Nelson George that they were "so dynamic that many established acts in town did not want to be caught on the same stage with them." Michael's high alto, impeccable phrasing, and vocal control were phenomenal. Befuddled by his uncanny talent, many mistook Michael for a middle-aged midget, which reportedly caused him distress. Introverted and reserved offstage, Michael morphed into a dynamo under the spotlight.

The Jackson 5 regularly opened for A-list talent. Michael got a priceless education from watching the likes of Jackie Wilson, James Brown, Sam & Dave, Etta

above JOSEPH WALTER JACKSON, THE CONTROVERSIAL PATRIARCH OF THE FAMILY, PICTURED IN DECEMBER 1972 AT AGE FORTY-THREE, THREE YEARS AFTER THE JACKSON 5 FIRST STORMED THE CHARTS WITH "I WANT YOU BACK." MICHAEL HAD A LIFELONG FEAR OF, AND AVERSION TO, HIS HARD-DRIVING FATHER.

A PUBLICITY PORTRAIT OF THE JACKSON 5 FROM THE MID-1960S, WHEN THE GROUP HAD ALREADY HONED THEIR SKILLS TO THE POINT THAT THEY INTIMIDATED MORE ESTABLISHED ARTISTS.

James, and Gladys Knight in their heyday. "I'd stare at their feet, the way they held their arms, the way they gripped a microphone, trying to decipher what they were doing and why they were doing it," Michael reminisced in his 1988 autobiography *Moonwalk*. "After studying James Brown from the wings, I knew every step, every grunt, every spin and turn."

BELOW THE SURFACE

On the surface the Jackson family appeared to be the model of working-class upward mobility. But behind the scenes, things may not have been so rosy. According to Michael, LaToya, and a number of third-party and

eyewitness accounts, Joe was a menacing figure capable of physical violence and emotional cruelty. (LaToya also claimed in her 1991 tell-all that there was sexual abuse.) Joe was allegedly extraordinarily insensitive to his sons' psychological needs. Michael recalls, "This was in Chicago, New York, Indiana, Philadelphia, all over the country. I'd be sleeping and I'd hear my father. 'Get up! There's a show!'"

Biographer Randy Taraborrelli alleges that Joe beat Michael and his siblings with whatever objects were handy: belts, whips, even refrigerator handles. The children were also well aware of Joe's numerous sexual infidelities. Sam Moore of the R&B duo Sam & Dave

above MICHAEL SHAKES HANDS WITH TELEVISION HOST ED SULLIVAN IN 1969.

22

recollects Joe locking young Michael in a closet at a show while he went carousing. Michael claimed in a 1993 interview with Oprah Winfrey that he became so disgusted and frightened of Joe that he would throw up in his mouth when his father approached.

Although Joe Jackson admits striking his children, he vehemently denies violently beating them. "I think children should fear their parents more," he told Taraborrelli in 1978. "It's good when they fear you a little. It's good for them, and it's good for the parents too." Other Jackson siblings, including Janet, refute the idea that any abuse occurred in the household. It's difficult to ascertain what the truth is, if there is a singular truth, about Joe Jackson. Whatever the case, Michael clearly developed a profound aversion to his father, although he also freely credited Joe with helping develop his talent. Michael carried that aversion into adulthood.

above DESPITE THEIR PICTURE-PERFECT IMAGE, THERE WAS A DARK SIDE TO THE JACKSONS' EARLY SUCCESS. *opposite* MICHAEL'S MUSICAL TIMING WAS SO IMPECCABLE THAT HE WAS OCCASIONALLY MISTAKEN FOR A VERY SMALL ADULT.

CLIMBING THE LADDER

In the summer of 1967, the Jackson 5 took the stage at the prestigious Amateur Night at the Apollo Theater in Harlem. The Jackson 5 won and were invited back for paid gigs. But what the group really wanted was a recording contract. In the 1960s, Detroit label Motown had racked up a string of monumental hit artists like Smokey Robinson & the Miracles, the Temptations, and the Supremes. CEO Berry Gordy had a great track record for finding and developing young black talent so that their success would "cross over" to white audiences.

The Jackson 5—managed by father Joe and his business partner, a lawyer named Richard Arons—had no direct "in" to Motown. Instead, they landed a deal with Gordon Keith's Gary-based record label Steeltown. They recorded two songs that made minor regional noise: "Big Boy" (backed with "You've Changed") and "We Don't Have to Be Over 21" (with "Jam Session" on the flipside). Motown star Gladys Knight, who became an early supporter after seeing the Jacksons perform at Chicago's Regal Theater in 1968, unsuccessfully lobbied Berry Gordy to audition the boys. Canadian Motown artist Bobby Taylor took a different tactic. He encouraged the boys to come to Detroit and arranged to film an audition tape for Gordy, who was in Los Angeles at the time. The Jacksons drove their Volkswagen to Detroit and dazzled Motown staffer Ralph Seltzer and Gordy's assistant

Suzanne DePasse. Two days later, Gordy offered Joe a recording contract. He signed it in the office without reading it or consulting a lawyer.

By 1968, Motown had already begun moving its base of operations to the West Coast. Michael and Jermaine were sent to live with label superstar Diana Ross in Los Angeles for a month while the rest of the family went house-hunting. Plucked out of his inner-city surroundings and dropped into a new magic kingdom, Michael was thrilled. "We were awestruck by California; trees had oranges and leaves on them in the middle of winter," he recalled in *Moonwalk*. "There were palm trees and beautiful sunsets, and the weather was so warm. Every day was special." Ross had recently left the Supremes and was about to launch her solo career; it appears that Michael developed something of an obsession with the superstar. Though Ross was not present much to guide or mentor the young singer, he imitated her singing and performance style as he began to craft his own version of stardom.

Gordy began to develop the Jackson 5. He turned to songwriter-producers—Deke Richards, Freddie Perren, and Fonce Mizell—to remodel a hit originally intended for Gladys Knight. "Give it the Frankie Lymon treatment," Gordy instructed, according to *The Encyclopedia of Record Producers*. "'The little guy who lost his girl' kind of thing, and we'll use it with the kids." Gordy himself joined the creative team. As a producer foursome called the Corporation, they tailored "I Want You Back" for

DIANA ROSS WAS GIVEN SOLE CREDIT FOR DISCOVERING
THE JACKSON 5. IN FACT, IT WAS BOBBY TAYLOR'S
EFFORTS THAT BROUGHT THE BOYS TO
MOTOWN'S ATTENTION.

the Jackson 5. They beefed up the backing vocals in the doo-wop soul style of Sly and the Family Stone's "Dance to the Music." The Jacksons were not necessarily tight harmony singers, so vocals and instruments had to be overdubbed repeatedly. The producers worked long hours to fine-tune the boys' phonetics and enunciation. At $10,000, it was an expensive production—three times what Motown would typically spend on a single.

To heighten anticipation for the release, Motown fudged the group's backstory. Superstar Diana Ross, not Bobby Taylor, would get sole credit for discovering the Jackson 5. The boys could not diverge from this script in press interviews. To amplify his cute factor, Michael was instructed to tell the press that he was eight, not ten. Although telling this white lie clearly perplexed him, he masked his feelings. "I figured out at an early age that if someone said something about me that wasn't true, it was a lie," Michael said later to Taraborrelli. "But if someone said something about my *image* that wasn't true, then it was okay. Because then it wasn't a lie, it was public relations." For her part, Ross introduced her protégés at a gala party held at the swanky Beverly Hills nightclub Daisy.

Diana Ross Presents the Jackson 5 hit the stores in December 1969 at the tail end of a tumultuous decade of social unrest. The effervescent song "I Want You Back" was a superb showcase for Michael's soaring, pristine vocals, and it soared to the top of the charts. Jon Landau of *Rolling Stone* went so far as to call its release

"one of the most fortuitous events in the recent history of pop music."

At age eleven, Michael Jackson had himself a number one commercial and critical hit. But while other children played, Michael worked long hours, earning money that he hardly ever saw. "My childhood was completely taken away from me," Jackson reflected when accepting the Grammy Legend Award in February 1993, "There was no Christmas, there was [sic] no birthdays, it was not a normal childhood, no normal pleasures of childhood—those were exchanged for hard work, struggle, and pain, and eventually material and professional success. But at an awful price, I cannot recreate that part of my life."

Whether Michael's gloomy account of his childhood was entirely accurate is something we may never know; he often blurred fact and fiction. But he would obsessively spend his life trying to recreate a mythic sense of childlike wonderment he had never known.

opposite A JANUARY 1971 PUBLICITY PHOTO OF THE JACKSON 5. CLOCKWISE FROM BOTTOM LEFT: MICHAEL (SEATED), TITO, JACKIE, JERMAINE, AND MARLON. *above* THE JACKSONS' FIRST ALBUM WITH MOTOWN, *DIANA ROSS PRESENTS THE JACKSON 5*, WAS RELEASED IN 1969.

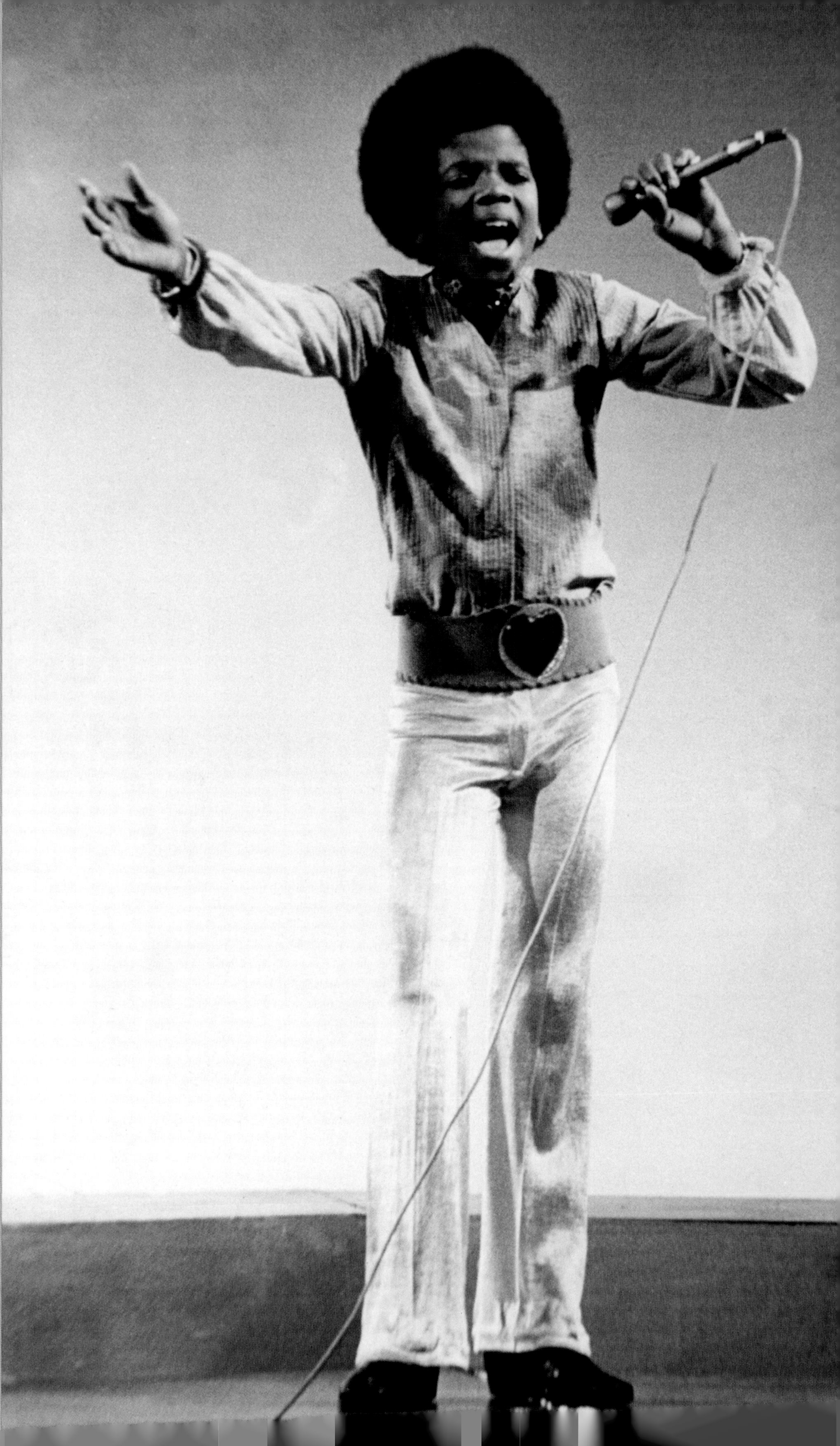

CHAPTER TWO

A PERFECT STAR

"IS IT HIS SUNSHINE SMILE? OR IS IT HIS DREAMY CHOCOLATE-BROWN EYES? OR COULD IT BE THE SWINGING WAY HE DANCES? WHATEVER IT IS MICHAEL JACKSON HAS— IT MAKES HIM A STAR AND IT MAKES HIM MARVELOUS!"

–*The editors of* Tiger Beat *magazine, 1972*

In 1970, eleven-year-old Michael Jackson was a big fan of crossover film star Sidney Poitier; he had memorized lines from Poitier movies *Blackboard Jungle* and *Lilies of the Field.* He had a thing for animals, too, although his mother, Katherine, wasn't fond of his pet white mice and snakes. The posters taped to his bedroom wall showed Motown R&B groups like the Supremes and Rare Earth, and a pinup of the white British soul siren Lulu, famous for her title track theme to Poitier's 1967 film *To Sir, With Love.*

Michael also dug classical music, easy listening, and rock. Crooner Johnny Mathis, soul man Ray Charles, and bluesy rockers Three Dog Night were special favorites. "I just about flipped when I heard 'Mama Told Me Not to Come' for the first time," young Michael gushed in the pages of *Right On!* magazine. "I sat there by the radio for forty-five minutes before the disc jockey played it

opposite WITH THEIR PERFECTLY COIFFED AFROS, FLUID VOCAL HARMONIES, AND UNISON DANCE MOVES, MICHAEL AND THE REST OF THE JACKSON 5 PUT A NEW, WHOLESOME SPIN ON THE IMAGE OF BLACK FAMILIES IN THE 1970S.

again. Talk about White Soul, Three Dog Night sure has it!"

Michael's early eclectic tastes—spanning pop, R&B, soul, easy listening, classical, rock, and musical theater—would later be key to the crossover success of his landmark solo albums *Off the Wall* and *Thriller*. But in the early '70s, Michael was being custom molded into the perfect teen superstar.

"SOUL BUBBLEGUM"

The prolific Jackson 5 released three back-to-back albums in 1970: *ABC*, *Third Album*, and *The Jackson 5 Christmas Album*. In an unprecedented feat, their first four singles went to number one. Catchy if simplistic "ABC" knocked the Beatles' "Let It Be" off the charts on

April 25. Zestful follow-up "The Love You Save" pushed aside the Fab Four's sorrowful "The Long and Winding Road" on June 27. Fans saw a softer side of the Jackson 5 with the sentimental heart-warmer "I'll Be There;" it coasted to the top October 17.

In the early 1970s, popular R&B musicians like Curtis Mayfield and Marvin Gaye boldly sang about their disillusionment over the Vietnam War, inner-city decline, and other social conditions. The sound of black music was getting darker, moodier. In marked contrast, the Jackson 5 sound was buoyant, giddy, wholesome. Berry Gordy called it "soul bubblegum." Michael was becoming the most advanced child singer of his generation, a commanding and skillful song interpreter. Michael impressed producer Freddie Perren in the

above THE JACKSON 5 ATTEND THE NAACP ANNUAL IMAGE AWARDS SHOW AT THE AMBASSADOR HOTEL IN HOLLYWOOD, NOVEMBER 1970. THE BOYS FROM GARY WERE RIDING HIGH: THEY HAD FOUR HIT ALBUMS AND FOUR NUMBER ONE SONGS IN THEIR DEBUT YEAR. *opposite* IN THIS PUBLICITY PHOTO FROM 1971, A YOUTHFUL MICHAEL WEARS A MICKEY MOUSE SHIRT.

THIRTEEN-YEAR-OLD MICHAEL LOOKS ADORABLE IN
A PHOTO SHOOT FROM JUNE 1971. HE HAS REASON TO
SMILE: THE JACKSON 5 BALLAD "MAYBE TOMORROW"
WAS A CHART HIT AROUND THIS TIME.

studio. "I would have him do the song," Perren recalled to biographer Nelson George, "and by the time we got to the end, it sounded so good, he had improved the performance so much, that I would have him go back to the beginning . . . With every take he got better." The pace of recording at Motown was furious: Michael would learn the songs, either in the studio or in the Motown office, and record them the same day. He could memorize three songs in a single hour. Over the course of the seven years they spent at Motown, the Jackson 5 recorded nearly five hundred songs, though only two hundred or so were ever released to the public.

Berry Gordy had found a group that would help woo the rising black teenybopper market. "There had never been soul idols for clean black teens before (only sportsmen and Martin Luther King)," music critic Simon Frith observed in his 1978 book *Sound Effects*. Ex-Disney staffer and Capitol Records employee Fred Rice had previously handled merchandising for pop supergroups like the Beatles and the Monkees. Berry Gordy realized he could bring in big bucks if he licensed the Jackson 5 image. He hired Rice to create Jackson 5 commodities in exchange for 25 percent of the gross on items sold.

JACKSONMANIA

Rice designed a heart-shaped, circle-enclosed Jackson 5 logo; it became a memorable visual trademark. He also came up with a Jackson 5 soul mate kit that you could order off the back of the *ABC* album cover: send for it

above MICHAEL HAD A LOVE FOR ANIMALS FROM AN EARLY AGE, ALTHOUGH HIS MOTHER WASN'T ALWAYS A FAN OF THE PETS HE KEPT.

CARTOON STILL

The Jackson 5 were so popular in the early
1970s that they had their own Saturday
morning cartoon series, *The Jackson 5ive*.
It started in September 1971 and ran for two
years. The animators added two dancing mice,
Ray and Charles, and a pink snake named
Rosey as additional characters, since fans
knew Michael Jackson was a pet lover
in real life.

POSTER

This promotional ad for the Jackson 5's single
"ABC" ran in a music industry publication. The
group was a reliable hit machine for Motown
for several years.

left MICHAEL WAS THE CONSUMMATE
OBSERVER, IMITATING ESTABLISHED
PERFORMERS AS A YOUNG CHILD.
opposite A POWERHOUSE ON STAGE,
MICHAEL WAS INTROVERTED IN PRIVATE.

A PENSIVE PORTRAIT OF MICHAEL AT THE
PEAK OF JACKSONMANIA. THE CHAOTIC FAN
FRENZY SOMETIMES OVERWHELMED HIM.

in the mail and you'd receive an autographed glossy photo, poster, writing pad, and *TCB,* a Jackson 5 newsletter magazine. Jackson 5 pens, lunchboxes, stickers, t-shirts, towels, and fridge magnets were right around the corner. While introspectively sitting in a corner on a break from working, Michael would color and sketch on a pad; Motown even auctioned off autographed copies of his doodles to the highest bidder in the pages of teen magazines.

Jacksonmania was a mass phenomenon in which teen and pre-teen girls became hysterical in public at the very mention of the Jackson 5—similar to 1960s Beatlemania. By the summer of 1970, it was in full effect. The boys had started touring in May of that year, and their rousing live show broke attendance records at venues like the Los Angeles Forum. Michael was no doubt the main attraction: frenzied girls screamed so loud when he sang that it's reported he sometimes had to stop the show. And girls swooned and regularly fainted when designated heartthrob Jermaine moved a finger. Mob scenes formed outside hotel rooms and teen magazines promised insight into the boys' likes, dislikes, innermost thoughts, and astrology signs. When black teen magazine *Right On!* launched in October 1971, it devoted every monthly issue for two years to the Jackson 5.

Jacksonmania boosted sales, but it also curtailed the family's privacy. In late 1969, the *Map and Guide to the Fabulous Homes of the Stars* tourist brochure listed the

street address for the Jacksons' home in the Hollywood Hills. Pandemonium ensued. "They'd come around with cameras and sleeping bags . . . They'd jump the fence and sleep in the yard and try to get inside the house. It really got crazy," Michael told biographer Nelson George. The family eventually packed their bags and left Los Angeles altogether. They moved to the Encino area, shelling out $250,000 for a sprawling twelve-room gated estate on Hayvenhurst Avenue, where the Jackson family still resides as of the writing of this book. Fans still showed up at the gate.

As wistful tunes like 1971's "Never Can Say Goodbye" and "Maybe Tomorrow" climbed the charts, the Jackson 5 earned two Grammy nominations and graced the covers of magazines like *Sixteen, Life,* and *Rolling Stone*—a major feat for a black group, much less a teen one. The Jackson 5 had so permeated the culture, that in September 1971, they received their own Saturday

above IN 1972, "BEN," A BALLAD FROM THE FILM OF THE SAME NAME, BECAME MICHAEL'S FIRST SOLO HIT. THIS ORIGINAL RECORD COVER WAS SWITCHED OUT BECAUSE THE RATS WERE DEEMED TO BE TOO FRIGHTENING FOR RECORD BUYERS.

morning Rankin-Bass animated television show. Hired actors dubbed the voices; the boys had no creative input whatsoever. Little Michael loved seeing himself as a Saturday morning cartoon character—an early indication, you might say, of narcissism to come.

Clean-cut and polite almost to a fault, the Jackson 5 offered a positive vision of the black family unit in an era when drugs and crime were taking a serious toll on inner-city communities. In 1971 the U.S. Congressional Record recognized the Jackson 5 for being a symbol of pride for black youth and the group received the NAACP Image Award for Best Singing Group of the

Year. Early Jackson 5 fan club president Steve Manning told Nelson George that "the Jackson 5 were then a very timely group for black Americans . . . It was the time of the Afro and black pride. Never before had black teenagers had someone to idolize like that . . . The kids identified with them not as stars, but as contemporaries fulfilling their fantasies of stardom." On January 31, 1971, the boys made a triumphant return to Gary to give a special performance and receive the key to the city from Mayor Richard Hatcher.

BRANCHING OUT

In 1971, the Osmonds (a white family from Utah who had become a music supergroup) began to revamp their square image to keep pace with the Jackson 5. Their lead singer, Donny, kickstarted a lucrative solo career on Mike Curb's MGM Records label. Eager to compete, Motown released Michael's first solo album, *Got to Be There*, in January 1972; it was considered part of the Jackson 5 franchise. Produced by four separate production teams, Michael's album had a strong anchor in the soaring title track, a dramatic Burt Bacharach–style ballad originally intended for the Supremes. Michael had arrived as a solo artist.

In summer 1972, fourteen-year-old Michael recorded "Ben," an earnest ballad about a boy's love for a rat from the horror-schlock film of the same name. A huge hit, "Ben" skyrocketed to number one and picked up an Oscar nomination. Michael performed confidently at

above BY 1972, JACKSONMANIA WAS IN FULL EFFECT. *opposite (above)* MICHAEL AND LITTLE SISTER JANET POSE IN 1972. *opposite (below)* THE JACKSON 5 WERE A WELCOME CLEAN-CUT IMAGE FOR BLACK TEENS IN THE EARLY 1970S.

the Academy Awards telecast, sporting a bejeweled red shirt with a white butterfly collar and black pants with jeweled seams. Film star Charlton Heston introduced him as "a young man whose talent is mature but his age suggests that maybe he shouldn't even be up this late."

Michael delivered two more solo projects on Motown: 1973's *Music & Me* and 1975's *Forever Michael*, but neither fared well on the charts. Hits also began to dry up for the overexposed Jackson 5. They released four more U.S. albums on Motown in the early 1970s, including 1972's *Lookin' Through the Glass* and 1973's *Skywriter*. *GIT: Get It Together*, also released in 1973, spawned a number two hit nearly a year later in the punchy, funky single "Dancing Machine," which also became the title of their penultimate Motown album. Performing "Dancing Machine" on popular television program *Soul Train*, Michael debuted the robot, an android-like dance that he'd likely picked up from West Coast pop-lockers. Throughout his career, Michael helped mainstream urban dance by hiring street choreographers and adding breakdancing moves like locking and the moonwalk to his unique choreographic palette.

The Jackson 5 had great success in the '70s on the touring circuit. They hit the road extensively across the United States in 1970 and 1971, and branched out in 1972 with concerts throughout Europe, South America, and Japan, breaking attendance records and performing for the Queen Mother in the UK. In September 1973, they became the first black group to tour Australia and

New Zealand. In 1974, the Jackson 5 took their first trip to Africa. It was a profound experience for young Michael to glimpse a type of suffering and poverty he had never known, and it sparked a lifelong interest in charity and service. And in April 1974, the Jackson 5 played a unique series of shows at the MGM Grand Hotel in Las Vegas (including performances by sisters Janet and LaToya), breaking attendance records.

TOO MUCH OF A GOOD THING

But the Jacksons' success continued to have its downsides. In 1970, Michael and brother Marlon attended Gardner Street Elementary on Hawthorn Avenue in Los Angeles. Classmates recall how throngs of students would follow Michael and his teacher chaperone around

opposite (above) THE BOYS INDULGE IN A BASKETBALL GAME IN THIS PREVIOUSLY UNPUBLISHED PHOTO. *opposite (below)* MICHAEL PLAYS WITH A DOG DURING AN EARLY 1970S PHOTO SHOOT.
above BY 1972 MICHAEL HAD BEEN SELECTED FOR SOLO STARDOM AS MOTOWN TRIED TO COMPETE WITH THE OSMONDS' DONNY.

YEARBOOK

The Jacksons moved to Los Angeles from
Gary in the early 1970s, after signing to
Motown Records. The school-age boys
enrolled in the private, celebrity-friendly
Walton School after crowds of fans made
it difficult for them to study at public school.
This 1972 yearbook reproduction features
portraits and candid photos of Michael and
his brothers.

left OBSESSIVE FANS MADE PRIVACY FOR
MICHAEL AND HIS FAMILY DIFFICULT TO
ACHIEVE. *opposite* THIS CANDID PHOTO
DEPICTS A RELAXED, SMILING MICHAEL.

MICHAEL WAS ALREADY BECOMING WELL
KNOWN FOR HIS STYLISH OUTFITS BY THE TIME
THIS 1974 PHOTO WAS TAKEN.

the playground at recess. "We'd come out of the school and there'd be a bunch of kids waiting to take pictures and stuff like that. We stayed in that school a week. One week! That was all we could take," Michael claimed to Nelson George in 1984.

By seventh grade, Michael attended Emerson Junior High. After more mob scenes and even a death threat, Katherine enrolled her sons in the private and elite Walton School in Panorama City, known as a school appropriate for child performers and children of celebrities. The Jackson 5's grueling tour schedule, however, meant that the boys attended classes inconsistently. They were mostly educated by special tutors. Biographer Randy Taraborrelli claims that the Jackson boys—particularly

Michael—developed poor penmanship, grammar, and spelling, and a relatively poor grasp of world history due to their compromised education. Writer Dave Marsh went a step further, asserting that their spotty education meant "neither Michael nor his brothers ever acquired the kind of intellectual sophistication required to deal with the intricacies of wealth and fame."

Fan hysteria was another dark side to the Jacksons' fame. Encounters with raving fans often crossed the line into real physical danger. In London, the boys were confronted with dangerous mob scenes: girls dug their nails into the boys' skin and pulled at their hair. Michael later said to *Rolling Stone* reporter Gerri Hirshey, "You feel like you're spaghetti among thousands of hands. They're

above THE JACKSONS ATTEND THE GRAMMY AWARDS ON MARCH 5, 1974 AT THE HOLLYWOOD PALLADIUM.

just ripping you and pulling your hair and you feel that [at] any moment you're just going to break." In 1988's *Moonwalk*, Michael asserted that he still had physical scars on his body from those early days.

In a 1977 *NME* magazine interview, the young Michael reminisced and nervously giggled about a particular Jackson 5 in-store promotional appearance in San Francisco in which the out-of-control fans shattered a store window. "It sounded like an earthquake. Three girls got their throats cut and a boy got his head cut," remembered Michael. "There was blood all over the place, it was so bad. It's dangerous and frightening when it gets like that. I don't want things to get that bad . . . little children getting hurt and everything."

Writer Dave Marsh discusses this story in his prescient 1985 book *Trapped: Michael Jackson and the Crossover Dream*. He mentions that the *Chicago Tribune* reported this curious event in 1974, asserting that while all the other band members panicked, Michael did not. Instead, he froze, much like the robot he portrayed in "Dancing Machine," in an attempt to convince the hysterical fans that he might be a store mannequin. Marsh saw this gesture as a bizarre and disturbing coping mechanism—and perhaps a clue to Michael's lifelong fascination with mannequins and his future paranoia and obsession with security.

In Marsh's book, brother Tito recalled how Michael's entire personality began to change on The Jackson 5's heavily mobbed 1972 UK tour: "Michael was being pulled every which way on that tour in London," he said. "He just seemed to disappear and it was scary."

above DANCING WAS A KEY INGREDIENT OF THE JACKSONS' STAGE SHOW. MICHAEL BECAME KNOWN FOR HIS INNOVATIVE, ELECTRIFYING DANCE MOVES.

MICHAEL TAKES THE STAGE IN 1975 ON *THE MUSIC THING*,
A TELEVISION SHOW HOSTED BY DICK CLARK.

CHAPTER THREE

LIVING OFF THE WALL

"ONCE THE MUSIC PLAYS, IT CREATES ME. THE INSTRUMENTS MOVE ME, THROUGH ME, THEY CONTROL ME. SOMETIMES I'M UNCONTROLLABLE AND IT JUST HAPPENS—BOOM, BOOM, BOOM!—ONCE IT GETS INSIDE YOU."

—*Michael Jackson in* Creem *magazine, June 1983*

By 1975, the Jackson 5's creativity had stalled. Slick, string-laden disco had grabbed the baton from smooth '70s soul. Joe Jackson's business relationship with Motown had become strained. As the boys' de-facto manager, alongside lawyer Richard Arons, Joe frequently butted heads with Berry Gordy. Motown focused too much on Diana Ross' film career, Joe argued, and in the process had continually underpromoted the Jackson 5's albums. Motown fanatically micromanaged the boys' press interviews. The Jacksons were not allowed to veer from the script, nor were they permitted to discuss "adult" matters like politics or drugs. They had very little voice of their own.

Joe also wanted to renegotiate the boys' draconian recording contract, which he had signed without legal advice. The Jackson 5 had never been granted freedom on Motown to write or produce their own material. They were often told what to sing

opposite BY NOVEMBER 1976, EIGHTEEN-YEAR-OLD MICHAEL WAS GRADUALLY DEVELOPING HIS SONGWRITING TALENTS AND WAS BECOMING KNOWN AS A SOLO SINGER AND DANCER.

and how to sing it: at fourteen, Michael complained to Gordy that he wanted more freedom in the way he recorded his vocals. "For a long time I was very obedient and wouldn't say anything about it," Michael confided in *Moonwalk*. "Finally it reached a point where I got fed up with being told exactly how to sing." While an artist like Stevie Wonder had artistic freedom to come up with an iconoclastic album like *Innervisions*, the Jacksons were force-fed tepid material like 1973's flimsy *Skywriter*.

In the music industry, songwriters who own the publishing rights to their material earn a significant amount of income each time their songs are performed or played publicly; artists who do not write their own material do not earn income from publishing. The Jacksons contractually did not own any part of the publishing rights to any of their songs and they were not happy about it. Being able to write and produce meant economic freedom.

MOVING ON

In the summer of 1975, the Jackson 5 packed their bags and signed a lucrative new deal with Epic Records, headed by label president Ron Alexenburg. Epic was a division of CBS Records, then under the supervision of president Walter Yetnikoff, who would become a key player in Michael's future success. The Jacksons' brash move to Epic infuriated Motown, who saw it as a deliberate breach of contract. A fierce legal battle ensued—

above SINCE 1972, THE JACKSONS HAD TOURED THE WORLD, PLAYING TO PACKED HOUSES. THIS 1977 PHOTO DEPICTS THE GROUP STANDING OUTSIDE THE HAMMERSMITH ODEON VENUE IN LONDON. THE JACKSONS ALSO PERFORMED AT THE QUEEN'S SILVER JUBILEE THAT SUMMER. *opposite* THE JACKSONS SPORT SNAZZY SUITS FOR THIS PROMOTIONAL PHOTO FROM THEIR SHORT-LIVED 1976-1977 TELEVISION VARIETY SHOW, *THE JACKSONS*.

which would not be fully resolved until 1980—with Motown retaining the Jackson 5 trademark and ultimately pocketing $600,000 in damages. Backed into a corner, the group renamed itself the Jacksons.

There were some additional snafus. Jermaine had married Berry Gordy's daughter Hazel in 1973. Faced with personal and professional loyalties, Jermaine stayed behind at Motown to pursue his solo career. Younger brother Randy replaced him. The Jacksons were also required to let their existing Motown contract expire before they could begin working for Epic. That would take eight months. In 1976, while they waited, Joe signed his boys up for a Jacksons CBS television variety show that would debut in July. Michael was unhappy. He saw the lightweight series as a "dumb move"—many a pop star had ruined his career by hosting a variety television show. Nonetheless, he agreed to do it out of a sense of family loyalty. The show ran for a season but was cancelled the following year due to poor ratings.

Epic Records proved a mixed bag. As part of their deal, the Jacksons had been promised greater creative control but Yetnikoff balked. The boys had no songwriting or producing track record: at best, the label would agree to let them contribute three tracks on each album. Alexenberg assigned them Philly soul mavericks Kenneth Gamble and Leon Huff, famous for their work with the Stylistics and Harold Melvin and the Bluenotes.

The album they produced, 1976's *The Jacksons*, regrettably spawned only one hit: the chipper "Enjoy

Yourself." From a historical standpoint *The Jacksons* is mostly noteworthy because Michael, eighteen years old, contributed one of his first ever songwriting attempts on the lightweight midtempo "Blues Away." Michael also shares writing credit with Tito on the slick but unmemorable "Style of Life." Gamble and Huff also produced the Jacksons' 1977 follow-up, *Goin' Places*. It made even less of a splash on the charts, but Michael's developing writing style was showcased again, to better effect, on the pulsing disco foot-stomper "Different Kind of Lady."

Michael claimed to have learned a great deal about songwriting from observing masters like Gamble and Huff during this time period. An early fan of MGM musicals, Michael had a strong interest in the development of the song itself, especially with regard to melody and arrangement.

---

opposite AS A TEENAGER, MICHAEL JACKSON DEVELOPED HIS WRITING SKILLS BY PENNING SONGS ON THE JACKSONS' EPIC RECORDS RELEASES *THE JACKSONS, GOIN' PLACES,* AND *DESTINY.* THESE EARLY ATTEMPTS PREPARED HIM FOR THE MONUMENTAL SUCCESS OF HIS 1979 SOLO EFFORT, *OFF THE WALL. above* MICHAEL IS DRIPPING WET AFTER COMPETING AT THE FIRST (AND LAST) ANNUAL ROCK 'N' ROLL SPORTS CLASSIC, IN 1978 IN LOS ANGELES.

Because he was unable to read or notate music, Michael often sang ideas and concepts into tape recorders. He then translated those ideas as completely as possible to the musicians he rehearsed with or to producers in the recording studio. He also claimed that songs came to him in dreams.

FEELING THE EFFECTS

In 1977, Michael Jackson was nineteen years old. He had undergone puberty in the public eye and was no longer the precocious cherub that he'd been at the start of his career. You had to search a lot harder to find him in the teen magazines; younger brother Randy fulfilled the cuteness quotient for the Jacksons. Over the years, Michael had become lanky and slightly effeminate. He giggled a lot in interviews. His singing voice had broken some time ago, although he retained a high, feathery tenor.

Always shy, Michael had become exponentially withdrawn. One probable cause: teenage Michael had become demoralized by the sudden appearance of acne. "I became subconsciously scarred by this . . . I got very shy and became embarrassed to meet people. The effect on me was so bad that it messed up my whole personality," he

above DESPITE HIS COMMERCIAL AND ARTISTIC SUCCESSES, THE TEENAGE MICHAEL BECAME INCREASINGLY ISOLATED WHEN OFF-STAGE. *opposite* DESPITE HIS OBVIOUS GOOD LOOKS, MICHAEL WORRIED ABOUT ACNE AND THE SIZE OF HIS NOSE.

MICHAEL JACKSON PERFORMING AT
NASSAU COLISEUM IN UNIONDALE, NEW YORK ON
NOVEMBER 8, 1979, WITH THE JACKSON 5.

later wrote in *Moonwalk*. Compounding his adolescent concerns was a deep shame about his features. Michael often discussed how his father regularly insulted him by making fun of the size of his nose. "Big Nose" was the taunt of choice, Michael alleged in *Living with Michael Jackson*, the infamous 2003 documentary by journalist Martin Bashir. "And on top of it, you got to go onstage . . . in front of hundreds of thousands of people, and just, God, it's just hard. I would've been happier wearing a mask."

One could argue that is exactly what Michael did as his career unfolded: he learned to mask his face by radically altering his features through plastic surgeries and

other procedures. In the wake of his death, many doctors surmised that at some time during his development—likely during his teenage years—Michael developed body dysmorphic disorder, a paralyzing psychosomatic condition in which the sufferer becomes preoccupied by perceived physical imperfection. The sufferer then obsessively tries to transform his body, losing perspective on how he actually looks to the outside world, leading to depression, anxiety, and withdrawal, among other symptoms.

In the late 1970s, reporters sometimes expressed frustration that teenage Michael wasn't forthcoming in responses to their questions. He still lived at home

above IN SWITZERLAND FOR A PERFORMANCE IN FEBRUARY 1979.

and remained deeply committed to his Jehovah's Witness faith. He ate very little, had a lithe frame, and purported to be a strict vegetarian. Some writers painted him as naïve and sheltered, even shallow. In a 1978 profile in *Crawdaddy* magazine, Michael is interviewed in a restaurant. He eats with his fingers. Unfamiliar with quiche, he reaches over and digs his fingers into a plate of it. In a 1979 profile in music magazine *Melody Maker*, Michael, sitting next to his sister Janet, instructs the interviewer to direct all questions to his sister, who then repeats the question back to Michael. Writer Leonard Pitts Jr. goes so far as to link Michael to the boy in the plastic bubble,

the infamously cocooned youngster with an immune disorder that forced him to live in total isolation. In a later interview with biographer Mark Bego, Michael likened himself to "a hemophiliac who can't afford to be scratched in any way."

All of the Jackson siblings grew up in a strict, conservative, and possibly repressive household. But each of Michael's brothers found personal freedom by getting married at an early age. Unwed Michael still lived at his parents' Hayvenhurst complex, and remained there until he turned twenty-nine. By the close of the '70s, Michael had been romantically linked to a few women: Maureen McCormick of *The Brady Bunch*, actress Tatum O'Neal, and Broadway star Stephanie Mills. But these did not appear to be more than platonic friendships. Rumors flew about Jackson's sexual preference. *Jet* magazine printed that he might be dating "Never Can Say Goodbye" songwriter Clifton Davis; there were rumors that he was taking hormones and undergoing a sex change.

Acting offered Jackson a form of desperately needed escape from these whispers—the chance to become someone else. Though a reported star turn in *The Frankie Lymon Story* never materialized, Jackson signed on to play the Scarecrow opposite Diana Ross' Dorothy in the film version of the Broadway musical *The Wiz*. Filming took place in New York in the summer of 1977; Michael and sister LaToya rented a pricey thirty-seventh-floor apartment on Sutton Place.

above JACKSON'S FIRST—AND ONLY—MAJOR ACTING ROLE IN A FEATURE FILM CAME IN 1978 WHEN HE PLAYED THE SCARECROW IN SIDNEY LUMET'S BLACK-THEMED MOVIE VERSION OF THE BROADWAY STAGE MUSICAL *THE WIZ*, OPPOSITE DIANA ROSS. "IT SHOWED ME HOW I CAN BELIEVE IN MYSELF IN A WAY I NEVER COULD BEFORE," HE SAID OF HIS EXPERIENCE WORKING ON THE FILM.

ALONG WITH CELEBRITIES SUCH AS JANE FONDA AND
THE VILLAGE PEOPLE, MICHAEL AND HIS FAMILY HAD
BECOME 1970S ICONS.

Jackson reportedly left the set each day still caked in makeup, refusing to take it off.

While staying in New York, Jackson latched on to a ragtag group of celebrity pals that included Andy Warhol and Liza Minnelli. He regularly attended swanky parties at Studio 54, the legendary exclusive disco. "I love the feeling, the excitement, the props coming down, and the balcony," he gushed in British documentary *The Rise and Fall of Studio 54*. "It's a good time." Famed writer and Studio 54 regular Truman Capote recalled that Michael and LaToya "were often escorted by actress Liza Minnelli and always taken to the basement," where sex and drugs flowed freely. LaToya claims that she and Michael turned down the drugs offered to them. Capote

more or less confirmed this: he reported that the most Michael would do was watch sex—perhaps he studied the bodies moving in the same way he once studied James Brown's footwork in the wings.

INDEPENDENT AND ON HIS WAY

In 1978, the Jacksons, now managed by Joe working in concert with Ron Weisner and Freddy DeMann, were finally granted the opportunity to write and produce their own album, *Destiny*. The results were nothing short of spectacular. Michael contributed to many of the songs, including the hit second single "Shake Your Body (Down to the Ground)," a blend of lethally funky horns, groovy bass, and ethereal falsetto.

opposite (above) MICHAEL EMBRACED HIS ROLE AS THE SCARECROW SO COMPLETELY, HE REFUSED TO REMOVE HIS MAKE UP AT THE END OF THE DAY. *opposite (below)* WHILE FILMING *THE WIZ*, MICHAEL AND SISTER LATOYA LIVED THE NEW YORK CELEBRITY LIFESTYLE. *above* MICHAEL PERFORMS IN NEW ORLEANS WHILE ON THE JACKSONS' DESTINY TOUR.

Jackson turned twenty-one in 1979. *The Wiz* had been a commercial and critical disappointment, though critics gave thumbs up to his limber performance as the Scarecrow. Jackson was ready to record a solo album for Epic Records. While working on the film set, Jackson developed a solid working relationship with the music supervisor and orchestrator, Quincy Jones. Jones had played trumpet with the legendary jazz star Dizzy Gillespie and had arranged songs for Ray Charles before making waves as a film composer. Jackson and Jones first met at Sammy Davis Jr.'s house in the early 1970s, but Jones had written off young Michael as "just a bubblegum singer." Jones told *Time Out* magazine in 1988, "I knew he had a lot of soul, a lot of talent, and I could feel something there but I never felt he had ever really let it go." Jackson mentioned to Jones that he was looking to hire a record producer; intrigued by Jackson's talent, discipline, and ambition on the set, he volunteered to do the job.

Quincy Jones claimed the concept behind 1979's *Off the Wall* was that "it was time to grow up, not to be a bubblegum singer anymore, to go out and feel everything you're supposed to feel at twenty-one years old." On the album cover, Jackson's black casual tux with white shirt—a suave look suggested by managers DeMann and Weisner—suggests a self-confident maturity. It also connected him back to song and dance men like Sammy Davis Jr. and Fred Astaire who had paved the way for him.

The songs on *Off the Wall* are uniformly strong; in contrast to many pop albums, there's very little filler. Englishman Rod Temperton, who'd penned hits for the disco outfit Heatwave, delivered jazzy disco-funk tunes with irresistibly clever pop hooks, like the title track and "Rock With You." Jackson wrote "Workin' Day and Night," a deeply funky groove with complex, layered percussion and sharp brass from Jerry Hey's Seawind Horns. The exhilarating "Don't Stop Til You Get Enough" is all swirling, symphonic strings and basslines supporting Jackson's falsetto melodies. "She's Out of My Life" is wistful, sentimental; the Stevie Wonder–penned "I Can't Help It" is achingly romantic; Paul McCartney's "Girlfriend" is tinged with reggae. Michael's singing throughout the album is daring, personal, and unique—full of the vocal ticks, squeals, and yelps that would become his trademark.

opposite ON STAGE WITH THE JACKSONS DURING THE DESTINY TOUR. *above* MICHAEL AND MARLON JACKSON VISIT WITH PRODUCER QUINCY JONES AT THE BROWN DERBY IN HOLLYWOOD.

Off the Wall is an ecstatic, exhilarating pop soul album—considered by many to be one of the greatest albums ever released. Critic Gavin Martin referred to it as "the final summation of the great disco party." The album produced four hit singles and spent eight months in the Top 10.

Jackson had desperately hoped to cross over into the pop charts with *Off the Wall*. He was nominated for only one Grammy, however, in the R&B category. He won the award, but chose not to attend the ceremony. He later said in a 1983 *Creem* interview, "I wouldn't be happy doing just one kind of music or label ourselves. I like doing something for everybody . . . I don't like our music to be labeled. Labels are like . . . racism." Jackson couldn't stand the thought of being pigeonholed.

Newly twenty-one with a hit album under his belt, Jackson decided to take matters into his own hands and assert his freedom. He fired his father Joe as manager—though he retained the services of co-managers DeMann and Weisner. Then, he hired the brash young lawyer John Branca. Using the commercial success of *Off the Wall* as leverage, Jackson worked to renegotiate his solo recording deal with Epic. In the process, he secured the highest royalty rate for any artist in the music industry. If his next solo album project were to succeed financially, he stood to make an inordinate amount of money.

Michael Jackson started off the 1970s as a child star under his father's overbearing authority. As the decade came to a close, he emerged as a young man on his way to becoming an independent, grown-up superstar.

---

above THE JACKSONS HORSE AROUND BACKSTAGE AT THE NASSAU COLISEUM IN 1980.

BY THE CLOSE OF THE 1970S, JACKSON WAS
A WELL-ESTABLISHED SOLO STAR

CHAPTER FOUR

THRILLS
AND CHILLS

"GROWING UP AS A YOUNG BLACK KID IN A
[SOUTH AFRICAN] TOWNSHIP, YOU EITHER DREAMED
OF BEING A FREEDOM FIGHTER OR BEING MICHAEL
JACKSON. IT WAS AS SIMPLE AS THAT."

–South African R&B artist Loyiso Bala in Billboard *magazine, July 2009*

H ad Jackson never recorded another album after *Off the Wall*, his place
in music history would have still been assured. In 1980, the Jacksons
had received a highly prized star on the Hollywood Walk of Fame. And
a year later, John Rockwell of the *New York Times* would praise Jackson as "the finest
young male pop singer of any race or style."

Released in October 1980, the Jacksons' *Triumph* album, which climbed to
number one on the R&B charts, is as vital and exciting as Jackson's solo *Off the
Wall*. The brothers once again served as producers and writers; it's arguably the most
cohesive album of their career. "This Place Hotel," written by Michael, is a theatrical
disco stomper with swirling classical strings and ghoulish special effects, a preview
of sounds we'd later hear on *Thriller*. The weird lyrics, a jumble of disconnected
images about heartbreak, evil, wicked women, and staring faces, may, in retrospect,

opposite IN 1981, JACKSON WAS RIDING HIGH AFTER THE SUCCESS OF *OFF
THE WALL* AND THE JACKSONS' *TRIUMPH*.

with Motown. They used those funds to experiment with music video, then a new format. Bruce Gowers and Robert Abel were hired to direct the special effects–heavy video for *Triumph*'s lead single "Can You Feel It." In the clip, the Jacksons play skyscraper-tall messiahs who have supernatural powers to spread glowing gold inspiration down to the multicultural masses on the ground below. "Can You Feel It" is fun—but it's also incredibly self-aggrandizing. In some ways it's a reminder of how deeply rooted the Jackson family was in evangelical religion. It's also the first time we see evidence of Jackson's savior complex, that condition where an individual can become preoccupied with fantasies of endless unchecked power and, conversely, victimhood and martyrdom. It wasn't the last time Jackson would play a glowing, God-like spiritual figure bestowing charity upon the world below. Many Michael Jackson fans do indeed believe he was an inspirational figure for them, if not at that level.

have been a clue that Jackson's real-life paranoia and fear of prying eyes was growing.

"It seems like when you're under pressure you find some kind of escapism to make up for that," he told journalist Sylvie Simmons in *Creem* in 1983. "Because the road is a lot of tensions: work, interviews, fans grabbing you, everybody wants a piece of you, you're always busy . . . It's like you're in a goldfish bowl and they're always watching you."

With Epic Records, the Jacksons received bigger promotional and marketing budgets than they'd had

The Jacksons also received significant tour support from Epic. They'd been on the road off and on since 1977. During that time, the brothers had taken their live act to new heights. Reviews of their Triumph Tour, which kicked off July 1981, rarely failed to mention Jackson's show-stopping command of the stage. While he'd always been a dynamite performer, he was now being hailed as a spinning, kicking, yelping, dazzling force of nature, as electrifying as the show's high-wattage special effects and pyrotechnics.

above OFF THE WALL CEMENTED JACKSON AS A COMMERCIAL AND CRITICAL SUCCESS.
opposite (above) JACKSON STEALS A RELAXED MOMENT IN 1981. BY THE EARLY 1980S, MANY CRITICS FELT HE HAD LEFT BEHIND HIS "CUTE" JACKSON 5 IMAGE TO BECOME A SOLO POP STAR OF FORMIDABLE POWER. *opposite (below)* FRESH FROM THE SUCCESS OF OFF THE WALL, HE WOULD DOMINATE THE POP CHARTS IN A MATTER OF MONTHS WITH 1982'S THRILLER.

Jackson continued to write and produce for others, working with sister LaToya in 1980. In October 1982, he wrote and produced the Top 10 hit "Muscles" for Diana Ross—a titillating ode to the glories of the male physique. When rumors arose about his sexuality as a result, Jackson tried to quell the gossip by reporting that the song was named after his pet snake, also called Muscles.

BACK IN THE STUDIO

In the summer of 1982, Jackson reteamed with Quincy Jones at Westlake Studios in Los Angeles to record the narration for the audiobook of Steven Spielberg's sci-fi blockbuster film *E.T.: The Extra-Terrestrial.* Just as he had once emoted to a rat in "Ben," Jackson now sang his heart out to a fictional alien on the sugary ballad

"Someone in the Dark." A huge *E.T.* fan, Jackson reportedly cried throughout the recording, perhaps seeing himself in the heartwarming story of a misunderstood alien stranded in a strange world. Due to contractual disputes, however, the storybook album was pulled from store shelves.

Jackson described himself as a "fantasy fanatic." In press interviews in 1982, he used the word *magic* to describe everything and everyone. Like film director Spielberg, Jackson was addicted to spectacular entertainment: art should be big, thrilling, jolting, full of panache and pizzazz. What was true for the movies could be true for music.

After *Off the Wall,* Quincy Jones told *Billboard* magazine, "we were kicking booty and fearless, ready to do anything." Armed with a $750,000 recording budget, they began the three-month recording process for Jackson's second Epic solo album, *Thriller,* at Westlake Studios. *Thriller* mixed pop, rock, soft rock, quietly stormy R&B, and more. It seemed to have something for every conceivable taste, and it must have come close, because after its release in December 1982, seven of the album's nine songs hit the top of the charts. "P.Y.T.," written by Rod Temperton, is an electro-funk finger-snapper, polished to a smooth veneer. "Human Nature" is a soft rock confection with a Jackson vocal so shimmering and fluttery it seems to evaporate as you listen to it. "Wanna Be Startin' Somethin'," a euphoric funk-jam written by Jackson, is a series of paranoid musings about

above A SELF-PROCLAIMED "FANTASY FANATIC," JACKSON LOVED THE MAGIC AND THEATRICS OF DISNEY THROUGHOUT HIS LIFE.

being used and preyed upon: he sings about becoming a vegetable and a buffet where "they eat of you" before the song climaxes into a heavenly chant from Manu Dibango's 1972 "Soul Makossa" disco classic.

Three key songs on *Thriller* became all-time pop music classics. Second single "Billie Jean" is a catchy, forboding tale of an obsessed fan waging a paternity suit. The lean, minimalist song hit the top of the pop- and black-singles charts simultaneously. Jackson claimed "Billie Jean" was about a particularly obsessive female fan whose bizarre letters caused him frequent nightmares. Quincy Jones could not believe innocent Jackson had penned such a sinister, darkly ambiguous tune. Jackson enlisted British ad man Steve Barron to direct the video: the pop star sports a funky black tuxedo while dancing down a sidewalk that magically lights up when he moves. Like magic, Jackson appears to vanish when a roving paparazzo tries to snap his photo.

Three months after "Billie Jean" broke, Jackson gave a landmark performance of the song on *Motown 25: Yesterday, Today, Forever*, the label's anniversary event featuring a wide array of Motown stars. Sporting a sequined shirt and socks and a black jacket and fedora, Jackson performed a high-energy greatest-hits medley with his brothers before launching into a solo performance of "Billie Jean." Starting with a nonchalant fling of his fedora to the floor, Jackson shows off many of the moves that would become his trademarks: he kicks and pushes his leg into the air, he spins around like a top and

lands stopped, on his toes. And he debuts the moonwalk, a seemingly magical backward two-footed glide that he'd picked up from breakdance choreographers Geron "Casper" Candidate, Cooley Jackson, and Jeffrey Daniel several years prior. When it was broadcast on television in May 1983, even Fred Astaire called Jackson to praise him as "one hell of a mover."

Thriller's third single "Beat It" is a driving antiviolence anthem featuring muscular rock guitar by Eddie Van Halen. Jackson saw a McDonald's commercial that had a look and feel he wanted to approximate for the video. He hunted down the director of the commercial, Bob Giraldi, and they came up with a *West Side*

above JACKSON WOWS THE CROWD AND MAKES HISTORY AS HE PERFORMS AT THE MOTOWN ANNIVERSARY CONCERT, *MOTOWN 25: YESTERDAY, TODAY, FOREVER* IN 1983.

Story concept about rival street gangs who find unity in dance. With invigorating choreography by Michael Peters, famous for his work on the Broadway musical *Dreamgirls*, Jackson sported a red leather jacket covered in zippers that would become one of his fashion trademarks. Jackson, the former Three Dog Night fan, gravitated to rock guitars and rock musicians for the rest of his career, working with musical icons like Mick Jagger, Freddie Mercury, and Slash of Guns N' Roses.

But it was the video for *Thriller*'s title track, a campy spoof of B-movie thrills and chills written by Rod Temperton and featuring a monologue by B-movie horror star Vincent Price, that changed the game. Jackson had always had a fondness for John Carpenter's 1978

film *Halloween* and he wanted to work with John Landis, director of 1981 horror-comedy *An American Werewolf in London*. What they ended up with is a delirious seventeen-minute short film chock-full of special effects. Wearing a now-classic angular red leather jacket designed by Deborah Landis, Jackson plays a "nice guy" on a romantic date. The moon comes out from the clouds and Jackson confesses, "I'm not like other guys." Jackson then morphs into a werewolf and goes on a destructive rampage—until we realize Jackson and his date are simply watching a movie. It's not real. Outside the movie theater, Jackson suddenly transforms into a creepy zombie and performs a group dance number with other zombies, also choreographed by Michael Peters.

opposite (above) MICHAEL JACKSON ON STAGE IN THE EARLY 1980S. *opposite (below)* OVER THE YEARS, JACKSON COLLABORATED WITH MANY ROCK MUSICIANS, INCLUDING THE BEATLES' PAUL MCCARTNEY. *above* JACKSON STEALS A SOLITARY MOMENT.

"I just loooooved becoming a monster," Jackson told *TV Guide* in 1999, "Because it gave me a chance to pretty much become someone else. It was just fun hiding behind this mask and just really letting this part of you, your body or your feelings out, but hiding behind a different character." The video plays on the idea: who is the real Michael Jackson? Is it the shy, nice guy who will do no harm? Or is there a monster, something evil, lurking behind the mask? That becomes the question of Michael Jackson's entire career.

At its peak, *Thriller* was selling more than 600,000 copies per week; it became the number one selling album of all time, selling nearly 50 million copies (topped in the U.S. market only by the compilation *The Eagles' Greatest Hits*). It remained on the album charts for two years. *Thriller* rejuvenated the entire music industry. Jackson

picked up seven Grammy Awards, including Album of the Year and an additional award for his contribution to the *E.T.* storybook. Epic Records had heavily researched audience demographics and promoted *Thriller* across all markets to achieve maximum exposure. Released in time for Christmas, Jackson also released a behind-the-scenes video, *Making Michael Jackson's Thriller*, that quickly became the biggest-selling music home video of all time.

With *Thriller* Jackson became an overnight sex symbol. His trademark look became a single jewel-encrusted white glove alongside black pants with gleaming white socks. Jackson said to *TV Guide*: "The glove was just—I thought one was cooler than two. I love to accent movement. The eye goes to where the white is—you know, the glove. And the feet, if you're

above A STILL FROM JACKSON'S 1983 VIDEO FOR "THRILLER." HOLLYWOOD EFFECTS WIZARD RICK BAKER CREATED THE HORROR-FILM COSTUMES.

THE EXTRAVAGANT LONG-FORM VIDEO FOR "THRILLER"
COST $1 MILLION, NEARLY FIFTY TIMES THE USUAL COST
OF A MUSIC VIDEO. *AN AMERICAN WEREWOLF IN LONDON*
DIRECTOR JONATHAN LANDIS HELMED THE PRODUCTION.

POSTER

A promotional poster for Michael Jackson's 1983 "Thriller" video. Jackson was a fan of the horror film *Halloween*. He hired *An American Werewolf in London* director John Landis to film the ambitious short film. It would change the face of music videos.

PRESS RELEASE

The press release from CBS detailing Jackson's triumphant night at the Grammys. He took home eight awards on February 28, 1984: Record of the Year and Best Pop Vocal Performance, Male ("Beat It"); Album of the Year, Producer of the Year, and Best Pop Vocal Performance (*Thriller*); Best Recording for Children ("E.T. The Extra-Terrestrial"); Best R&B Vocal Performance, Male and Best R&B Song ("Billie Jean").

left JACKSON APPEARS EBULLIENT AT THE OPENING OF THE STAGE MUSICAL *DREAMGIRLS* IN 1983. *opposite* JACKSON MADE USE OF THEATRICAL COSTUMING IN HIS STAGE PERFORMANCES.

JACKSON SHARES THE GRAMMY LIMELIGHT WITH
PRODUCER QUINCY JONES.

dancing, you can put an exclamation point on your movement if it has a bit of light on it. So I wore the white socks." Jackson also began wearing embroidered military jackets and epaulets, a look he cribbed from rock-star friend Adam Ant, who had been wearing historical costumes as part of his pop-star act for years. *Thriller*'s album cover, photographed by Dick Zimmerman with hair and makeup by Karen Faye, portrays Jackson lying on his side, staring seductively into a camera, sporting a pristine white suit and curly processed hair with a perfect Superman curl dangling down from his forehead. Jackson looked slightly androgynous, feminized. *New York Times* writer Margo Jefferson would call the album cover the '80s version of a Hollywood studio portrait.

Thriller had a major influence on black pride and self-esteem—how people around the world perceived black people and, just as importantly, how black people began to perceive themselves. Writer Greg Tate describes how "black people cherished *Thriller's* breakthrough as if it were their own battering ram against the barricades of American apartheid." In 1982, MTV was a relatively new television format that played wall-to-wall videos; it so happened that most of those music videos were by white pop and rock artists. The station refused to play videos by R&B artists like singer Rick James; they were deemed to be inappropriate for MTV's desired pop/rock demographic. In the convoluted racial history of the music industry, black musicians have often been shut out of the mainstream while white artists, who draw

above NOW A GLOBALLY RECOGNIZED SUPERSTAR, JACKSON HAD EVEN LESS PRIVACY. HE SOMETIMES DESCRIBED HIMSELF AS A GOLDFISH LIVING IN A BOWL.

-singles charts. "Billie Jean" and "Beat It" also dominated white and black radio stations at the same time, ensuring *Thriller*'s crossover success. On December 10, 1983, Jackson broke Elvis' and the Beatles' records for the most top ten singles to be released in a single year. Some writers felt that a seminal moment in black American history had been achieved. Quincy Jones said to *Time* magazine in 1984: "No doubt about it . . . He's taken us right up there where we belong. Black music had to play second fiddle for a long time, but its spirit is the whole motor of pop. Jackson has connected with every soul in the world."

THE MAN BEHIND THE SHOW

But how did Jackson handle all this success? On one hand, he craved privacy, hiding himself behind trademark aviator shades. On the other hand, Jackson was becoming increasingly addicted to the thrill of being the most desirable person on the planet. He recalled the success from *Thriller* as a "bittersweet time" in a 1999 *TV Guide* interview. The album had fallen short of his artistic expectations. "If I don't get exactly what I'm looking for," he said, "I get very depressed." While the public had been stunned speechless by his amazing appearance on the Motown twenty-fifth anniversary special, Jackson admitted that he was privately angry about the fact that he hadn't hovered on his toes the extra few seconds he'd been hoping for.

on or copy black styles, often reap greater financial and cultural rewards. When Elvis was widely crowned the King, many African-Americans felt that it would be next to impossible for a black artist to achieve that sort of title. Until Jackson came along.

After Yetnikoff threatened to pull all the label's videos from MTV unless they played Jackson's work, "Billie Jean" became the first video by a black artist to enter into heavy rotation on MTV, breaking the station's de facto race barrier and changing the way it programmed videos. Jackson became the first artist to hold the number one spots on *Billboard*'s rock-albums and rock-singles charts simultaneously, as well as the R&B-albums and

According to Yetnikoff, in his 2005 memoir *Howling at the Moon*, Jackson had a monomanical need for

above JACKSON HAD HIS FIRST SURGERY ON HIS NOSE IN 1979. OVER THE COURSE OF THE NEXT DECADE, HIS FACE WOULD CHANGE RADICALLY, FUELING ENDLESS MEDIA SPECULATION. *opposite* JACKSON'S THEATRICAL STAGE PRESENCE, MUSICAL PROWESS, AND FLAMBOYANT STYLE INSPIRED LEGIONS OF FANS.

JACKSON MADE NUMEROUS BOLD FASHION STATEMENTS
THROUGHOUT HIS CAREER, BUT NONE MORE ICONIC
THAN HIS SINGLE SEQUINED WHITE GLOVE.

constant success: "Michael's passion for world conquest was singular . . . Michael's drive bordered on the psychopathic. He lived, breathed, slept, dreamt and spoke of nothing but number-1 successes. He was possessed. He called me night and day for the latest figures. 'They're tremendous,' I'd say. 'They need to be more tremendous,' he'd reply."

In the spring of 1983, at the height of his success, Jackson impulsively fired his management team of Freddy DeMann and Ron Weisner. He hired Epic promotions executive Frank Dileo. Though some criticized such a rash move, Jackson's attorney John Branca said in *Time* in 1984: "Michael is very informed and aware of what is going on in his life, to an amazing degree."

When Yetnikoff threw a huge celebration for Jackson at the American Museum of Natural History in February 1984, Jackson spoke publicly, comparing artistic success with sales. "For the first time in my entire career I feel like I have accomplished something because I'm in the *Guinness Book of World Records*."

THE VICTORY TOUR

Jackson was also torn between his need to find freedom as a solo artist and the compunction to remain loyal to his increasingly needy family. In 1984, against his better judgment, he agreed to join his five brothers (Jermaine returned, having left Motown) for a new album, *Victory*, and a huge splashy tour sponsored by Pepsi. The frothy album, released on July 6, was critically maligned. But

the extravagant, mega-spectacular tour, which started in July and lasted until December, broke attendance records and grossed somewhere around $75 million. It was also the only chance to see Michael Jackson live that year because he did not tour to support *Thriller*.

Billed as the most lavish and expensive concert of all time, the Victory Tour boasted 3,300 multicolored lights; a 160-foot, five-story stage; five ten-foot monsters called Kreetons; and computer-controlled metal "spiders" created by Disney engineers. At one point in the show, Jackson appears to levitate and then disappears, much to the delight of throngs of screaming fans.

Behind the scenes, however, the Victory Tour was a fiasco of mismanagement and financial conflicts between event producers Joe and Katherine Jackson, flamboyant boxing promoter Don King, inexperienced replacement promoter Chuck Sullivan, and a litany of other cooks in the kitchen. These backstage conflicts

above A 1984 PHOTO DEPICTS JACKSON IN A TRADEMARK LOOK: EPAULETS, HAT, SHADES, AND A WHITE GLOVE.

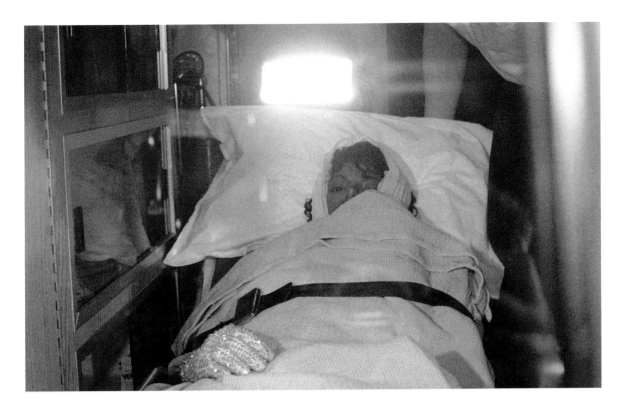

soon became public news. The Jacksons were criticized for overcharging for tickets and selling tickets in bundles of four, which all but guaranteed largely well-to-do white audiences. They were also widely criticized for ignoring black promoters who had supported them throughout their rise in the '70s. All this unwanted controversy and backstage bickering was personally embarrassing to Jackson. He donated all his proceeds from the tour to charity. At the last show, with no warning, he announced that it would be his last tour ever with his brothers. And, on that front, he kept his word.

THE PRICE OF THE TICKET

With *Thriller*, Jackson had grabbed the brass ring; he had attained stratospheric success and redefined the concept of celebrity. But the price of the ticket may have been too high.

In January 1984, Jackson was filming a Bob Giraldi–directed Pepsi commercial when a spark from the pyrotechnics caught his hair on fire. He suffered second- and third-degree burns on the top of his scalp. The news spread like wildfire and, ironically, created enormous buzz and anticipation for the advertisement when it aired. By all accounts, the incident piqued Jackson's lifelong curiosity with health issues. He became obsessed with details of what doctors do and how various experimental procedures work. It also may have been the start of his addiction to prescription painkillers.

Jackson's obsessions over personal security and privacy also continued. In November 1984, Jackson

opposite JACKSON EXITS THE STAGE IN THE LAST MOMENTS, OF THE LAST CONCERT, OF THE VICTORY TOUR. *above* JACKSON PEERS OUT FROM BANDAGES AFTER RECEIVING SECOND- AND THIRD-DEGREE BURNS ON HIS SCALP WHILE FILMING A PEPSI COMMERCIAL.

POSTER

A poster from the 1984 Victory Tour. After achieving major solo success with *Thriller*, Michael Jackson reluctantly went on the road with his brothers to support their *Victory* album. Pepsi served as the sponsor for the tour, which was billed as the most extravagant in history.

TICKET

A ticket to the first show of the 1984 Victory Tour. The tour kicked off at Arrowhead Stadium in Kansas City, Missouri, where the Jacksons played three sold-out shows. Approximately 45,000 people attended each night, demolishing attendance records for the city.

left JACKSON IN 1983. *opposite* PERFORMING WITH THE JACKSONS ON THE FIRST NIGHT OF THE VICTORY TOUR, JULY 7, 1984. AMAZINGLY, JACKSON DID NOT TOUR IN SUPPORT OF *THRILLER*.

boy who never grows old. The self-described fantasy fanatic also told *Rolling Stone* that he kept mannequins in his house and had long conversations with them. In an interview on the set of "Beat It," interviewer Tom Joyner asked Jackson to name his personal friends. There was a long pause; Jackson, hidden behind sunglasses, clearly had trouble answering the question. He first named his fans. When Joyner prompted him again to name "personal" friends, Jackson searched for a more substantial answer. He then answered, listing Quincy Jones, Jane Fonda, and Diana Ross. But these seemed like less-than-forthright answers. Rock-star friend Freddie Mercury once mentioned that Jackson rarely left his house during this period. And, apparently, when Jackson did leave the house, he usually went to Disneyland.

At the 1984 American Music Awards, Jackson appeared at awards shows with two dates: diminutive black child star Emmanuel Lewis on one arm and white actress Brooke Shields on the other—a curious combination that had people buzzing. By 1985, Jackson would make regular public appearances with his diapered chimpanzee Bubbles on his arm.

Jackson appeared to be a divided soul: on one hand he craved the spectacular excesses that came with his stardom. On the other, he portrayed himself as an ascetic who didn't drink, didn't smoke, wouldn't touch aspirin, took regular purgative enemas, and was too modest to speak about sex in interviews.

received his own star on the Hollywood Walk of Fame, but left the ceremony after only three minutes as he became panic-stricken about his safety in the crowd. "I hate to admit it . . ." he said to Mark Bego, "but I feel strange around everyday people. See my whole life has been onstage. And the impression I get of people is applause, standing ovations and running after you. In a crowd I'm afraid. Onstage I feel safe. If I could I would sleep on the stage. I'm serious."

As Jackson's popularity grew he retreated even further into his own world. He began talking about starring in a film version of *Peter Pan*: he had reportedly become fascinated by the J. M. Barrie story of the

above JACKSON PERFORMS IN DECEMBER 1984 IN LOS ANGELES. *opposite (above)* THROUGHOUT HIS LIFE, FAN ADORATION WAS JACKSON'S GREATEST LOVE AND GREATEST PAIN. *opposite (below)* FANS ARE WHIPPED INTO A FRENZY AS THEY ANTICIPATE JACKSON'S ARRIVAL IN LONDON.

A 1985 PORTRAIT SHOWS AN INTROSPECTIVE JACKSON. ALTHOUGH HE WAS AT THE HEIGHT OF HIS SUCCESS, RUMORS WERE ALREADY BEGINNING TO SWIRL ABOUT THE CHANGES IN HIS APPEARANCE.

During his *Thriller* days, it's reported that Jackson continued to go door-to-door in Los Angeles to sell the Jehovah's Witness publication *The Watchtower*. Due to his celebrity status, Jackson naturally wore a mask or disguise. Door after door would shut in his face. It seems that Jackson found the very idea of associating with everyday people who had the instant power to reject him—the most popular person on earth—personally humiliating. Even so, he remained devoted to his religious convictions. In March of 1983, the elders of the Jehovah's Witnesses came down hard on Jackson: they saw the "Thriller" video as a glorification of the occult. Jackson immediately responded with a public statement that he would never do anything like it again and issued a disclaimer that ran before the opening credits of the video.

Rumors had also started swirling about Jackson's face. He'd clearly had one or more nose jobs and his skin was noticeably lighter. Why was he wearing so much makeup? Why wouldn't he take his sunglasses off? What was he trying to hide? In April 1984, the *Sun* asked, "Is Jacko Wacko?" The British press had coined a phrase that would stick. Savage attacks on Jackson appeared in *Time, Wall Street Journal, The Nation, The New Republic, Washington Post,* and *The National Review.* Nation of Islam figurehead Louis Farrakhan even called Jackson "sissified." Comedians like Eddie Murphy and Joan Rivers endlessly parodied his growing racial and sexual ambiguity.

By September 1984, Jackson felt the need to respond the rumors and criticisms. In a bizarrely staged press conference, at which Jackson did not appear, Jackson's cigar-chomping manager Frank Dileo read from a prepared statement without removing his sunglasses:

"NO! I've never taken hormones to maintain my high voice.

NO! I've never had my cheekbones altered in any way.

NO! I've never had cosmetic surgery on my eyes.

YES! One day in the future I plan to get married and have a family. Any statements to the contrary are simply untrue."

This was the first of many occasions where Jackson had the chance to clarify his enigmatic behavior, but chose to create even more mystery.

above AT HIS MOTHER'S BIRTHDAY PARTY ON MAY 4, 1984. JACKSON HAD ALREADY HAD HIS FIRST COSMETIC SURGERY ON HIS NOSE IN 1979. DURING THE 1980S, HIS FACE CHANGED DRAMATICALLY.

BAD MOON RISING

"THIS OBSESSION WITH BIGNESS OBLITERATES THE ISSUE OF WHAT'S BEST, BURIES IT UNDER THE BANNER OF BIGGEST EVER. BEING BIGGEST IS A SETUP FOR BEING ECLIPSED."

–*Dave Marsh,* Trapped: Michael Jackson and the Crossover Dream, 1985

In the wake of *Thriller*, Michael Jackson had a lot on his plate. He produced and wrote songs for others in 1985, including the warmhearted "You're the One" for *Dreamgirls* star Jennifer Holliday and the toe-tapper "Eaten Alive" for Diana Ross (with Barry and Maurice Gibb).

Jackson became increasingly known for his charitable works. He had long been involved with social causes and, in the summer of 1984, President Ronald Reagan invited Jackson to the White House to honor him for an anti-drinking and driving campaign. Following British singer Bob Geldof's 1984 Band-Aid, a supergroup gathering of top British performers who recorded a hit song to raise money for African famine relief, Harry Belafonte and music manager Ken Kragen partnered on the idea to produce an American equivalent called USA for Africa. Michael Jackson and Lionel Richie collaborated on the songwriting.

opposite JACKSON, AGE TWENTY-NINE, POSES WITH HIS PET BOA CONSTRICTOR MUSCLES. HE CLAIMS TO HAVE WRITTEN THE 1982 DIANA ROSS HIT "MUSCLES" FOR HIS FAVORITE SNAKE. WHILE DOING AN INTERVIEW FOR *ROLLING STONE* IN 1983, HE DRAPED THE REPTILE AROUND THE INTERVIEWER. AT HIS NEVERLAND RANCH ZOO, MICHAEL HAD A HOUSE FOR REPTILES.

WE ARE HERE TO CHANGE THE WORLD.
GEORGE LUCAS present A 3-D MUSICAL MOTION PICTURE SPACE ADVENTURE.
Directed by FRANCIS COPPOLA starring MICHAEL JACKSON as CAPTAIN EO
PRESENTED BY THE EASTMAN KODAK COMPANY AT DISNEYLAND AND
WALT DISNEY WORLD EPCOT CENTER . . . AND NOWHERE ELSE IN THE UNIVERSE!

On the evening of January 28, 1985, after the American Music Awards, forty-five famous artists headed over to A&M's Lion Share Studios to record the song. Quincy Jones served as producer, and told the celebrities to check their egos at the door. The star-studded gathering was filmed for the official music video. Collaborators included Bob Dylan, Al Jarreau, Bruce Springsteen, Cyndi Lauper, and several Jackson siblings. Released in March to huge sales, "We Are the World" became the top-selling single of all time and won Grammys for Song of the Year, Record of the Year, Best Short Form Video, and Best Pop Group. As proceeds were earmarked for famine relief in

Africa, the song helped initiate a new era of charity rock, in which popular musicians mobilized to raise money or awareness for social causes. "We Are the World" helped cement Jackson's reputation as a humanitarian.

He hadn't lost his touch as a businessman, either. In August 1985, Jackson, working in concert with manager Frank Dileo and attorney John Branca, secured the purchase of the highly lucrative Associated Television Corporation (ATV) song publishing catalog, which contained the rights to the Beatles compositions written by John Lennon and Paul McCartney, in addition to hundreds of thousands of additional song copyrights. He paid $47.5 million, outbidding competitors that included Paul McCartney and Yoko Ono. It was a shrewd, and ruthless, business move. McCartney and Jackson were long-time friends who had collaborated on hot songs like "Girlfriend" and 1983's chart topper "Say, Say, Say." McCartney was, in fact, the one who first informed Jackson about the lucrative catalog; the young singer was simply willing to pay more than McCartney was for his own material. Some saw it as Jackson's scheme to dominate the Beatles by owning them. Jackson and McCartney never collaborated again.

In March 1986, Jackson signed a $15 million sponsorship deal with Pepsi, the most lucrative endorsement deal ever at the time. And by September, his friend Jeffrey Katzenberg, the head of Disney, convinced Jackson to star in Francis Ford Coppola's sci-fi adventure short film *Captain EO* to play at Epcot Center and Disney World.

above A 1986 PROMOTIONAL POSTER FOR *CAPTAIN EO*, A $30 MILLION 3-D SCI-FI FILM DIRECTED BY FRANCIS FORD COPPOLA AND EXECUTIVE PRODUCED BY GEORGE LUCAS. IT PLAYED AT DISNEY THEME PARKS LIKE EPCOT CENTER AND SPAWNED THE SONG "ANOTHER PART OF ME," WHICH WAS INCLUDED ON JACKSON'S 1987 *BAD* ALBUM.

MICHAEL JACKSON TAKES A MOMENT BEFORE
GOING ON STAGE AT LONDON'S WEMBLEY STADIUM
IN 1988, DURING THE BAD TOUR.

BY THE TIME MICHAEL JACKSON'S BAD TOUR STARTED IN 1987, HIS SKIN WAS SEVERAL SHADES LIGHTER THAN IT HAD BEEN JUST A FEW YEARS BEFORE.

THE MASK

Even as his career evolved, Jackson himself was transforming, right before the public's eyes. He'd already had several rhinoplasties (surgeries to alter the nose) by the mid-1980s, mostly the handiwork of his controversial plastic surgeon, Dr. Steven Hoefflin. The first, in 1979, was to straighten out his broken nose after a fall. Others appear to be vanity procedures. More surgical work had allegedly been done to his lips, nose, and cheekbones, and he had a cleft put in his chin. He heavily tweezed his eyebrows and wore a copious amount of pancake makeup. He also began to occasionally wear a surgical mask in public—possibly to hide scars or botched surgeries, or just for the effect. No statements were made to the press at the time to explain these visible changes. He would admit only to having two nose surgeries and adding the cleft in his chin.

From later court testimony, we now know that dermatologist Dr. Arnie Klein first saw Jackson as a patient in 1986. He immediately diagnosed the singer with discoid lupus, due to the presence of a signature butterfly rash on his face, and crusts that had formed on the burned area of his scalp as a result of the Pepsi commercial accident two years prior. A biopsy confirmed that diagnosis. Jackson also suffered from vitiligo, an autoimmune disorder that can cause hyper- or hypo-pigmentation of the skin, leaving the skin lighter or darker, blotchy, and even disfigured. Prolonged exposure to sunlight can be dangerous; this may explain Jackson's public use of umbrellas on sunny days. He may have used

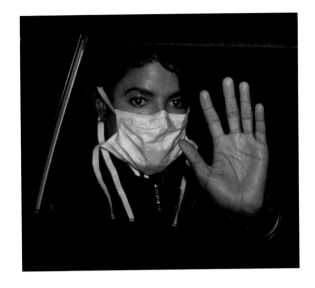

heavy makeup to even out his skin tone, and Klein started prescribing powerful bleaching creams in 1990.

Jackson, however, continued to keep quiet about his medical conditions and the extent of his cosmetic reconstructions—it was, after all, nobody's business but his own. Media controversy ensued. In 1987 the *New York Daily News* printed a three-part series called "Wizard of Odd." Readers could look at detailed before and after pictures of the singer with arrows and captions as guides. Jackson claimed to be bothered by the chatter, but he also saw controversy as a way to remain a talked-about figure of mass desire. "The bottom line is they don't *know*," he told biographer J. Randy Taraborrelli, "and everyone is going to continue searching to find out whether I'm gay, straight, or whatever . . . And the longer it takes to discover this the more famous I will be."

Jackson was threatened by two prospects: staying ahead of the competition, and staying on top. A crop of '80s music stars like Bobby Brown, El DeBarge, Terence

above WEARING ONE OF THE SURGICAL MASKS THAT LANDED HIM IN THE TABLOIDS, JACKSON WAVES FROM A LIMOUSINE IN LOS ANGELES IN 1988.

Trent D'Arby, Jermaine Stewart, MC Hammer—not to mention sister Janet, who landed her first successful solo album in 1986—all borrowed from Jackson's sound and look. But Jackson was most concerned with the status of R&B star Prince, the Minneapolis musician whose 1984 success with the *Purple Rain* soundtrack and film eclipsed the Jacksons' Victory Tour press. In 1984, *Right On!* magazine even devoted an issue to the question: "Who rules the music kingdom—Prince or Michael?"

By 1987, Prince had emerged as the critical favorite. His March release, the double album *Sign 'o' the Times*, was widely considered a sprawling musical masterpiece. Critic Barney Hoskins noted in *The Times*, "It was as if an extraordinary inversion of Jackson had crept up behind him and stolen his crown—an impish doppelganger whose campily erotic stage antics made Jackson look too squeaky-clean by half. Prince, moreover, did it all: wrote, sang, arranged, performed and produced music immediately more eclectic and challenging than anything Jackson had ever dreamt of."

UNLEASHING *BAD*

In January 1987, Jackson had begun recording the sessions for *Bad* with Quincy Jones again on board as producer. He was under intense pressure to top *Thriller's* success. Jackson reportedly affixed a piece of paper to his bathroom mirror. It read "100 million"—a daily reminder of his colossal sales goal. The recording sessions for *Bad* were far behind schedule. Jackson was in enormous conflict with himself to finish the record, obsessively discarding takes in the quest for artistic perfection. Rumor had it *Bad* would feature duets with hip-hop group Run-DMC and pop icon Barbra Streisand. Neither of the collaborations materialized. In December 1986, Quincy Jones arranged a meeting between Michael and Prince. That too went nowhere, but it at least inspired Jackson to put the pedal to the metal. It was still more than a year before *Bad* hit store shelves.

While recording *Bad*, Jackson seemed to enjoy stirring up controversy. He craved public attention. In September 1986, the *National Enquirer* had published photos of him lying with his arms crossed in a hyperbaric chamber. Rumors flew that he was sleeping in the chamber every night in a Walt Disney–like effort to become immortal. Jackson did not respond directly to the rumor. Many years later, in his 1993 live television interview with Oprah Winfrey, Jackson

above AT A PEPSI PUBLIC RELATIONS EVENT IN 1988; JACKSON SIGNED A HUGE ENDORSEMENT DEAL WITH PEPSI IN THE WAKE OF *THRILLER*'S PHENOMENAL SUCCESS. *opposite* WITH ONE OF HIS BACKING GUITARISTS ON TOUR IN LONDON, 1988.

MICHAEL JACKSON PERFORMS "THRILLER" AT WEMBLEY
STADIUM, LONDON, IN APRIL 1988. EVEN THOUGH *BAD*
CONTAINED MANY NEW HIT SONGS, AUDIENCES NEVER
LOST THEIR APPETITE FOR *THRILLER*'S SINGLES.

finally provided an explanation. He claimed that the photo was taken while he inspected a burn treatment center in the aftermath of his Pepsi incident. He was simply checking out the equipment and someone had casually taken a picture that leaked. Taraborrelli refutes this story. He says it was Jackson himself, acting in concert with manager Dileo, who hatched an elaborate scheme to plant the photo with *National Enquirer* and in the legit press. Jackson's harshest critics would point to a sinister root to these fabricated eccentricities: as in magic, if you throw up smoke and mirrors on the left, then you can get away with anything on the right.

Taraborrelli claims that Jackson gave Dileo a copy of a book about P. T. Barnum, the circus huckster who famously subscribed to the belief that a sucker is born every minute, and instructed him to study it, saying, "I want my whole career to be the greatest show on earth." In May 1987, rumor had it that Jackson, a huge fan of the 1980 David Lynch film *The Elephant Man*, had made a bid to buy the actual bones of the real-life elephant man, John Merrick, from the London Hospital Medical College for a reported $1 million. Taken together, these sorts of rumors turned Jackson into a laughing stock. Upon *Bad*'s September release, *NME* magazine was cheekily noting that Jackson "bathes in Perrier water and wants to build his own Buck House. He asked David Hockney to paint Diana Ross' face on the bottom of his swimming pool and he hopes to live until he's 150."

In his biography *Howling at the Moon*, CBS Records president Walter Yetnikoff called Jackson a "super-salesman of his own mystique." But Jackson was locked in a conflict that would have a tragic end. On one hand,

above AT MADISON SQUARE GARDEN, NEW YORK CITY, ON MARCH 3, 1988. HIS FIRST TOUR AS A SUPERSTAR SOLO ARTIST KICKED OFF IN SEPTEMBER 1987 IN YOKOHAMA, JAPAN. HE WENT ON TO PERFORM 123 CONCERTS OVER SIXTEEN MONTHS FOR 4.4 MILLION FANS; THE TOUR BROKE RECORDS BY GROSSING $125 MILLION.

TICKET

On March 3, 1988, Michael Jackson performed a sold-out concert at Madison Square Garden in New York City to benefit the United Negro Scholarship Fund. His first New York concert since 1984 was billed as a private affair and raised $600,000 for the organization. Pepsi sponsored the event and audience members wore free paper Pepsi hats.

NEWSLETTER

A fan club newsletter from the *Bad* era. Jackson had a deep, intimate connection with his legion of fans around the world.

PATENT

Jackson and his backup dancers created an unforgettable moment in the 1989 video for "Smooth Criminal" when they all stood in place and leaned forward at an uncanny angle. The effect was achieved with wires on film, but in 1993 Jackson tweaked it to work on stage. He obtained a patent to protect his concept of a special shoe that affixes to the stage to recreate the leaning effect live; it's a reminder of Jackson's competitive business savvy.

left A 1987 PUBLICITY STILL FROM *BAD*. JACKSON, MANAGER FRANK DILEO AND EPIC RECORDS COULD NOT AGREE ON AN ALBUM COVER; THEY CHOSE ONE FROM THIS SERIES OF PHOTOS, TAKEN AT THE VIDEO SHOOT FOR THE ALBUM'S TITLE TRACK. *opposite* ON STAGE IN CALIFORNIA, NOVEMBER 8, 1988.

he valued being considered extraordinary and a figure of universal desire. He craved the public spotlight, even if that spotlight had to be rigged through hoaxes. On the other hand, Jackson remained intrigued—and repulsed—by the concept of normalcy, that state of ordinariness he had no real conscious memory of. "I would don my disguise of fat suit, wig, beard, and glasses and head off to live in the land of everyday America," Jackson reminisced on beliefnet.com in 2000, "visiting shopping plazas and tract homes in the suburbs. I loved to set foot in all those houses and catch sight of the shag rugs and La-Z-Boy armchairs with kids playing Monopoly and grandmas baby-sitting and all those wonderfully ordinary and, to me, magical scenes of life. Many, I know, would argue that these things seem like no big deal. But to me they were positively fascinating."

Bad hit stores around Jackson's twenty-ninth birthday in August 1987. The hard aggressive sound and feel of hip-hop had begun to dominate popular music. To keep pace, Jackson adopted a new style—black leather, zippers, studs, buckles, chains. The album title itself was a nod to urban slang. Writer Barney Hoskins found all this surreal in his *Vogue* review. "One look at *Bad*'s cover, however, makes clear just how unreal Jackson's 'street' image really is," he wrote. "With his gossamer-delicate, surgically sculpted features, he looks like a beautiful Latin girl trapped inside an outfit from *Mad Max II*."

Jackson was the primary songwriter on *Bad*. The debut single, "I Just Can't Stop Loving You," went to number one on September 19; it's a creamy romantic duet with R&B singer Siedah Garrett. "Another Part of Me," from *Captain EO*, rides along a slick, sinuous jazz-funk groove. Chart-topping single "The Way You Make Me Feel" is a propulsive synthesizer dance track with a swinging melody that seems straight out of the Fred Astaire era. Throughout, Jackson's singing is gritty, aggressive, and more percussive than it's been before.

Bad received mixed critical reviews; some felt it was a lesser creative effort in comparison to *Thriller*. But commercially, it was a juggernaut, producing seven chart hits and five number ones. *Bad* ultimately sold more than 20 million copies and hit number one in thirty-five countries. Epic Records was relieved. *Bad* was "more than simply a new creative product," Yetnikoff claims in his memoirs, "it was a corporate

above JACKSON AND HIS BACKUP SINGER, SHERYL CROW, PERFORM A DUET DURING A CONCERT IN ROME IN MAY 1988.

AT THE SHERATON HOTEL IN NEW YORK CITY, APRIL 1988.
JACKSON'S DELICATE FEATURES BELIED THE NEW
URBAN IMAGE HE TRIED TO CREATE WITH *BAD*.

event." Jackson ended the year as *Forbes'* highest paid entertainer: he earned $97 million in 1987 and 1988, and he would earn $125 million in 1988 and 1989.

The videos from *Bad* were spectacular entertainments following in the footsteps of *Thriller*. CD bonus track "Leave Me Alone" is a delirious stop-motion ride through an amusement park of Jackson's own life. A direct retort to his critics to stop obsessing about him, it's a tongue-in-cheek send-up of the rumors that followed him since *Thriller*.

In the elegant film noir video for murder mystery "Smooth Criminal," directed by Colin Chilvers, Jackson plays a gangster dressed in a sharp white zoot suit, cavorting in a vintage nightclub. At one point in the video, Jackson and his dancers stand in place and lean their bodies forward in an angle that does not appear humanly possible. Viewers were puzzled: was this magical moment a trick of the camera or a supernatural new dance move? In fact, they used special cables to support the dancers: it was a graceful illusion, a trick of the eye not unlike his famous moonwalk. When he went on tour, Jackson needed to recreate the effect. He personally conceived and patented a special antigravity shoe with a hole in the heel. A peg comes through the floor that allows live dancers to lean toward the ground at uncanny angles.

No video from *Bad*, however, was more talked about than the eighteen-minute short film for the title

---

above IN JACKSON'S 1989 VIDEO FOR "SMOOTH CRIMINAL," HE DEVISED A MAGICAL MOVE, AN ANTIGRAVITY LEAN IN WHICH HE AND HIS DANCERS STAND IN PLACE AND LEAN FORWARD AT AN IMPOSSIBLE ANGLE. TO RECREATE THE EFFECT ON STAGE, JACKSON CREATED A PATENTED SHOE DESIGN: A HEEL CUTOUT FITS OVER A PEG THAT RISES OUT OF THE FLOOR TO HOLD THE DANCERS IN PLACE. *opposite* IN COSTUME FOR A LIVE PERFORMANCE OF "SMOOTH CRIMINAL" IN 1988.

track, the album's lead single. Directed by the acclaimed Martin Scorsese, with a $2 million budget, Jackson plays a prep school kid who has to defend his street credibility upon his return to his New York street roots. It ends with an exuberant dance number staged in the New York subway. While loved by many, the video was also a source of tremendous parody. *Village Voice* scribe Guy Trebay said, "There's no longer any question that Michael Jackson is America's preeminent geek."

The concern about whether Jackson was "manly" enough to play the thug in "Bad" was matched by the question as to whether he was black enough. While television's *The Cosby Show* portrayed a successful

black family who had not turned their back on their heritage to get ahead, many felt that the increasingly lighter-skinned Jackson was ashamed of his race. A debate brewed in the pages of the *Village Voice*, and writer Greg Tate weighed in: "Digging into our black nationalist bag, Jackson emerges a casualty of America's ongoing race war—another Negro gone mad because his mirror reports that his face does not conform to the Nordic ideal."

Critic Stanley Crouch countered Tate in the same paper, arguing that Jackson had every right to mold himself into whatever vision of blackness suited him. "The American dream," he said, "is actually the idea that an identity can be improvised and can function socially if it doesn't intrude upon the freedom of anyone else."

Before *Bad*, Jackson had never toured as a solo artist. He launched an eighteen-month, Pepsi-sponsored *Bad* tour in September 1987. The first stop was Japan, where he performed fourteen sold-out shows and picked up the nickname Typhoon Michael. That year, Jackson became the first American artist to have paid advertisements on Soviet television. And his concerts in Malaysia were cancelled because officials found it too difficult to control the crowds. He performed to 4.5 million fans in 120 countries around the world.

For all the talk that *Bad* felt like a corporate product rather than an artistic achievement, it also seems to have a human heart. Hit single "Man in the Mirror," written by Glen Ballard and Siedah Garrett, is a powerful and

above PERFORMING WITH THE FAMED RAT PACK ENTERTAINER SAMMY DAVIS JR. IN MONACO. *opposite* JACKSON FILMED THE 1987 "BAD" VIDEO IN THE GRAFFITI-FILLED HOYT-SCHERMERHORN SUBWAY STATION IN BROOKLYN, NEW YORK. THE EIGHTEEN-MINUTE VIDEO, WRITTEN BY RICHARD PRICE AND DIRECTED BY MARTIN SCORSESE, ATTEMPTED TO SHOW A TOUGHER, MORE URBAN SIDE OF JACKSON.

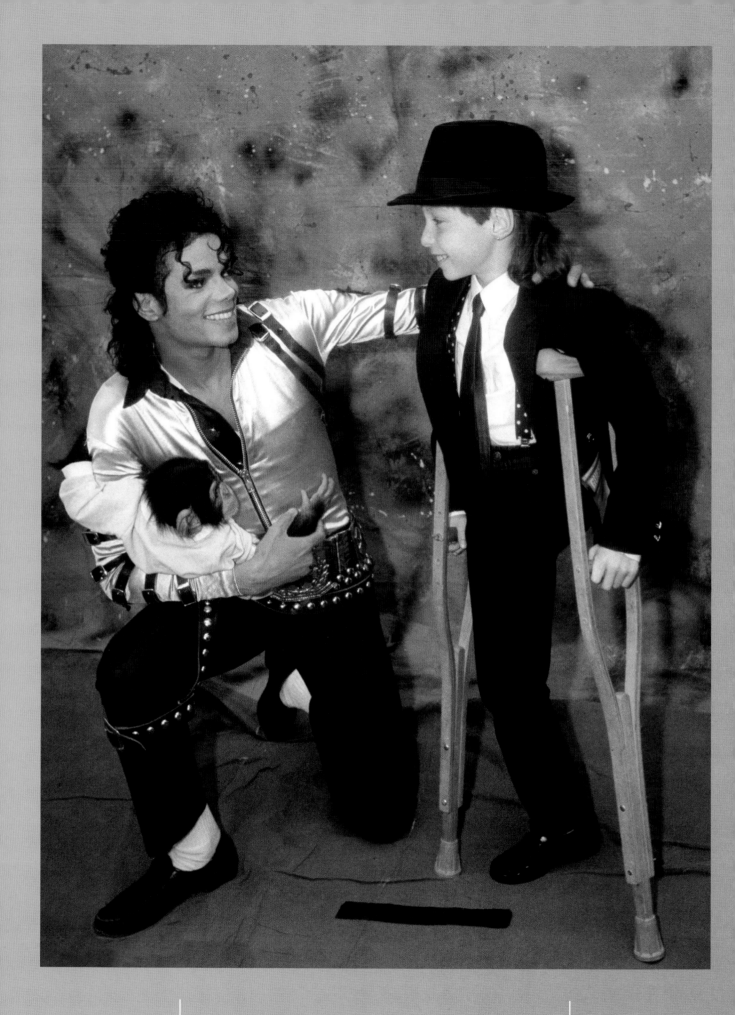

JACKSON BACKSTAGE WITH A CHIMPANZEE AND
ANDREW WIGGLESWORTH IN 1989. THE TEN-YEAR-OLD
BOY, WHO LOST HIS LEFT LEG TO A TUMOR, DREAMED
OF BECOMING A ROCK STAR.

moving inspirational anthem preaching that social change springs from the individual desire for self-transformation. Jackson's concept for the music video was a montage of scenes of global conflict culled from news reports. Jackson only appears in a brief scene at the end—a bold move for someone so highly visible. Furthermore, all proceeds from the track were donated to Camp Good Times for terminally ill patients. Continuing his humanitarian efforts in 1988, Jackson raised hundreds of thousands of dollars for the United Negro College Fund and many proceeds from his ongoing live concerts were earmarked for charitable causes.

Bad received four Grammy nominations that year. On the February telecast, Jackson performed a lip-synched version of "Man in the Mirror." At the song's close he began to sing live, caught up in the spirit of an impromptu moment that the broadcasters had not intended. He could clearly be heard ad-libbing the provocative lyrics: "black man got to change / white man got to change." It was an audacious moment, to be sure.

---

above JACKSON'S PET CHIMPANZEE BUBBLES, POSING WITH A STUFFED BUBBLES DOLL AND A PHOTO OF HIMSELF AND JACKSON, IN TOKYO IN 1987. BY THE MID-1980S, BRITISH TABLOIDS HAD BEGUN CALLING JACKSON "WACKO JACKO" BECAUSE OF HIS INCREASINGLY BIZARRE BEHAVIOR. RUMORS ABOUNDED THAT HE WAS SLEEPING IN OXYGEN CHAMBERS, THAT HE ENJOYED TALKING TO MANNEQUINS, AND THAT HE HAD AN ADDICTION TO PLASTIC SURGERY.

his abuse at any length—though it was hardly a revealing read. Jackson and Jackie's relationship soured when he stalled on reprinting the book. Jackson's lengthy and grueling Bad Tour culminated in January 1989 with the release of *Moonwalker*, a spectacular $27 million, sixty-minute film. Though video sales were enormous, Jackson was reportedly upset with Frank Dileo that he had not been able to secure a full theatrical release for the film.

NEVERLAND

In March 1988, a few months before his thirtieth birthday, Jackson moved out of his Encino home and purchased a sprawling 2,700-acre, $20 million California ranch in the Santa Ynez Valley, secluded far away from tabloids and paparazzi. He called the property Neverland, after Peter Pan's home.

A fantasyland of epic proportions, Neverland consisted of a main three-story house, bronze statues of young children, a complete train station with a working passenger train, a massive cinema complex, a full zoo with giraffes and llamas and other animals, and arcades. Jackson's stated concept was to build a home for himself and a retreat for ill and terminally ill children. The massive ranch, which cost $4 million a year to maintain, had intense twenty-four-hour security, including armed guards. "Becoming successful means that you become a prisoner," Jackson once told writer Paul Theroux.

Manager Frank Dileo had become so important to Jackson that his photo appeared in liner notes to *Bad* and

But *Bad* was shut out of its four Grammy nominations. Mary Hart of *Entertainment Tonight* referred to it as "the most unwelcomed comeback of the year." Jackson reportedly stormed out of the building, angered that he hadn't been rewarded for his efforts.

In 1988, Jackson released an autobiography, *Moonwalk*. He worked with editor Jackie Onassis and a series of ghostwriters. It became a number one *New York Times* bestseller. It was one of the first times Jackson spoke about

above A CLOSEUP OF JACKSON'S LIGHTENED SKIN, ON STAGE IN MONTPELLIER, FRANCE, 1988. *opposite* JACKSON HOSTS A 1989 BENEFIT FOR ST. VINCENT'S RESIDENCE, ONE OF THE MANY CHARITIES HE SUPPORTED OVER THE YEARS.

he made a cameo in the "Smooth Criminal" video. But in February 1989, Jackson fired him, with no stated reason. He hired Sandy Gallin as his manager the next year.

In June 1989, Jackson contributed vocals to the title track of *2300 Jackson Street*, a brand-new Jacksons album on Epic. It fared poorly on the charts; the brothers never recorded again as a group. In the coming years, Jackson would fall out with other business colleagues, including Walter Yetnikoff of CBS, confidant and colleague billionaire David Geffen, business manager Marshall Gelfand, and lawyer John Branca—though Jackson rehired him three years after firing him. Jackson never used Quincy Jones as a record producer again. And, when he moved out of his family's home into Neverland, he never officially let them know, nor did he invite them to the housewarming party.

By the spring of 1987, Jackson had also left the Jehovah's Witnesses, unable to reconcile his celebrity lifestyle and the church's demands. Without an active spiritual center, he seemed to have become increasingly isolated and alienated from the outside world.

Leaving the Jehovah's Witnesses allowed Jackson to begin experimenting with many of the decadent worldly things he had previously foresworn. The once staunch vegetarian craved Kentucky Fried Chicken and would request it (with the skin off) three times a day, as detailed in the list of food requests he submitted in September 2003 for service on his private charter plane. He ate McDonald's as well. He cursed. For someone who would not

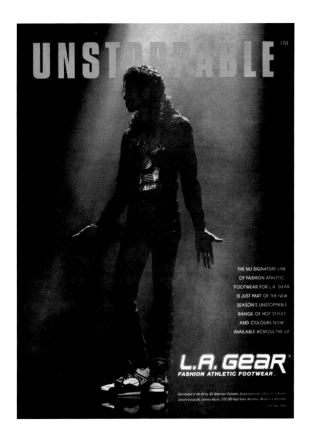

drink a sip of Pepsi even when endorsed by the company, he drank wine—a lot of wine—and many other types of liquors, often concealed in soda cans. When police raided his home in November 2003 with a search warrant, they found many open bottles, as well as a large amount of pornography—strange, for a man reportedly modest and shy about sex.

Coming clean about a KFC craving makes you seem more human, more normal. Although part of Michael Jackson was obsessed with seeing how normal people lived, another part didn't want to be perceived as normal or ordinary. There were clearly disparities in his persona, warring dualities. Who was the man behind the mask?

above A UK AD FOR THE LINE OF SNEAKERS JACKSON DESIGNED WITH L.A. GEAR, ONE OF HIS MANY LUCRATIVE ENDORSEMENT DEALS. *opposite* JACKSON'S STYLE LEANS TOWARD THE MILITARY ON A FLIGHT FROM SYDNEY TO MELBOURNE, AUSTRALIA, IN 1990.

CHAPTER SIX

LIVING DANGEROUSLY

"THERE'S A CERTAIN SENSE THAT ANIMALS AND CHILDREN HAVE THAT GIVES ME A CERTAIN CREATIVE JUICE, A CERTAIN FORCE THAT LATER ON IN ADULT-HOOD IS LOST BECAUSE OF THE CONDITIONING THAT HAPPENS IN THE WORLD . . . WHEN I SEE CHILDREN, I SEE THAT GOD HAS NOT YET GIVEN UP ON MAN."

–Michael Jackson in Ebony *magazine, May 1992*

Michael Jackson released only two solo albums in the ten years between 1980 and 1990. And yet he ruled the decade. At the start of the 1990s, *Vanity Fair* named him the Most Popular Artist in the History of Show Business, and President George Bush recognized him as Artist of the Decade at a White House ceremony.

By 1991, Jackson was spending little time at the palatial Neverland. After the Bad Tour, he spent nearly three years in and out of expensive recording studios putting finishing touches on the album that would ultimately become *Dangerous*. The Sony Corporation had purchased CBS Records in 1987, and record executive Tommy Mottola had replaced Walter Yetnikoff as music head by 1990. In 1991, Mottola

opposite MICHAEL PERFORMS AT LONDON'S WEMBLEY STADIUM IN 1992 ON THE DANGEROUS TOUR. HE PLAYED WEMBLEY, THE SECOND-LARGEST STADIUM IN EUROPE, MORE THAN FIFTEEN TIMES IN HIS CAREER.

re-signed Jackson to the most lucrative artist deal in music history. It was announced that he would launch the "Jackson Entertainment Complex," a fifty-fifty multimedia joint venture with Sony Software. Jackson would be expected to create films, theatrical shorts, television programs, and run his own boutique label. He reportedly received an $18 million advance for *Dangerous* and more than $108 million in total for successive future recordings. Given his high royalty rate and promised bonuses, he stood to earn $120 million if sales of his next album matched those of *Thriller*. This landmark deal made headlines, but it was a risky move for Jackson and for

CBS. Jackson had never starred in a successful film, nor had he developed artists for labels—and despite *Bad*'s success, it never approached *Thriller*'s numbers.

DANGEROUS

Jackson's new album *Dangerous* made a strong debut in November 1991. The album, produced by new jack swing pioneer Teddy Riley, Bill Bottrell, and Jackson himself, featured a mix of inspirational ballads and blocky, hard-edged grooves influenced by hip-hop. The cover was a surreal, enigmatic illustration of Jackson's eyes hidden behind a huge theatrical mask.

above JACKSON POSES WITH GUNS N' ROSES GUITARIST SLASH IN 1991, DURING THE FILMING OF THE JOHN LANDIS-DIRECTED VIDEO FOR THE HIT SINGLE "BLACK OR WHITE." MICHAEL HAD A LIFELONG INTEREST IN ROCK MUSIC AND OFTEN INVITED HEAVY METAL ARTISTS TO MAKE CAMEO APPEARANCES ON HIS RECORDS.

JACKSON IN BUCHAREST, WHERE HE FILMED THE HBO
SPECIAL, *DANGEROUS*. HE OFTEN HELPED DESIGN HIS
ECCENTRIC COSTUMES: ON THIS TOUR HE APPEARED AS
A MIX OF SUPERHERO, GENERAL, AND GLAM ROCKER.

Those peering eyes are surrounded by a variety of curious objects and hidden details intended to keep the public guessing.

Lead single "Black or White," a catchy if simplistic celebration of colorblindness and racial harmony, features a bright pop melody surrounded by swirling hard rock guitars played by Guns N' Roses guitarist Slash. On November 14, Jackson aired the song's eleven-minute video. Nearly 500 million people in twenty-seven countries watched as, in the contoversial final segment of the original video, Jackson morphed from a black panther through the use of computer-generated graphics and then aggressively danced on a car while grabbing his crotch, simulating masturbation, and breaking windows with a bat. Though the video seems tame by today's standards, it certainly got people talking at the time. Naturally, controversy fueled sales: "Black or White" became Jackson's biggest hit since "Billie Jean," staying on top of the pop charts for seven consecutive weeks. Jackson became the first artist to have number one pop hits in three different decades: the '70s, '80s, and '90s.

Second single "Remember the Time" shot to number three on the pop charts in February 1992. For the $4 million video, Jackson hired *Boyz 'n the Hood* director John Singleton and friends Magic Johnson, Eddie Murphy, and supermodel Iman. The spectacular clip

above ON THE FIRST LEG OF THE DANGEROUS TOUR, AT THE HIPPODROME DE VINCENNES IN FRANCE, SEPTEMBER 14, 1992.

was set in a mythical ancient Egypt. "Gone Too Soon," another one of the album's high points, is a touching, earnest ballad designed as a tribute to young AIDS victim Ryan White, whom Jackson had befriended.

At the end of June 1992, Jackson kicked off the Dangerous Tour in Munich, and stayed on the road on various legs of the tour until August 1993, though there were more than the usual number of cancellations, allegedly due to Jackson's throat problems and viruses. Many of the proceeds from the tour were earmarked for Jackson's Heal the World Foundation, a non-profit he launched "to improve the conditions for

children throughout the world" by providing medicine and other services.

In the latter half of 1992 and into 1993, Jackson seemed to be everywhere: he appeared at President Bill Clinton's inauguration, the NAACP's 25th Annual Image Awards, and the American Music Awards. And in October, cable television channel HBO aired the special *Michael Jackson Live in Bucharest: The Dangerous Tour.* Its depiction of hysterically screaming fans in a massive concert venue reminded American audiences of the size and loyalty of Jackson's audiences around the world. At the end of the show Jackson (or a body double) dons a

above LEAVING THE STAGE VIA JET PACK AT LONDON'S WEMBLEY STADIUM ON AUGUST 20, 1992.

TICKET

The European leg of Michael Jackson's acclaimed and extravagant Dangerous Tour kicked off at the 80,000-capacity Olympiastadion in Munich, Germany in June 1992. Sony threw a massive amusement park–style VIP party in Munich for Jackson right after opening night. The Dangerous Tour never reached the United States.

BACKSTAGE PASS

A 1992 official backstage guest pass from the Dangerous Tour. Each night Jackson left the stage by putting on a rocket jet pack and seemed to fly out of the auditorium. He used a body double for this exit stunt. FedEx had to use two freight jets to carry the scenery over to Europe, indicating how massive the tour was.

MASK

A rare collectible mask from the Dangerous Tour. Pop artist Mark Ryden created the enigmatic cover illustration for *Dangerous* on which the mask is based. "Michael wanted it to be mysterious, for people to interpret for themselves," Ryden has said.

left PERFORMING DURING THE SUPER BOWL XXVII HALFTIME SHOW ON JANUARY 31, 1993. *opposite* POURING HIS HEART OUT ON STAGE IN ROTTERDAM DURING THE DANGEROUS WORLD TOUR, 1992.

jet pack and flies out of the stadium. It's a stunning, magical disappearing act.

In January 1993, Jackson performed an electrifying set live at the Super Bowl XXVII Halftime Show at the Rose Bowl in Pasadena. It was broadcast to 1 billion viewers in seventy countries. The program drew the largest viewing audience in the history of American television and Jackson donated his hefty fee to the Heal the World Foundation.

A DIFFERENT KIND OF DANGEROUS

Once considered the ultimate functional family, the Jacksons had begun to air their dirty laundry in public. In September 1991, two months before *Dangerous* hit the stores, LaToya Jackson, who had already estranged herself from her family by posing for *Playboy*, released a tell-all book. In it she elaborated on Michael's admission in *Moonwalk* that their father Joe had physically and verbally abused his children, including Michael. She also alleged that her father sexually abused the oldest Jackson daughter, Maureen. The family tried to discredit LaToya by arguing that her husband, Jack Gordon, was using her to exploit them.

In November 1991, radio stations played a pre-release version of "Word to the Badd!!" an R&B track by Jermaine Jackson condemning his brother Michael for lightening his skin. Michael reportedly confronted Jermaine and convinced him to rework the lyrics for the song's final version. A year later, all of the Jackson family members, except LaToya, gave their blessing to the

above SURROUNDED BY FANS AFTER HIS HALFTIME PERFORMANCE AT THE SUPER BOWL ON JANUARY 31, 1993. *opposite* JACKSON LEAPS AMONG THE PYROTECHNICS DURING THE HALFTIME SHOW, WHICH DREW THE LARGEST VIEWING AUDIENCE IN AMERICAN HISTORY.

MICHAEL JACKSON AND HIS DATE TO THE GRAMMY
AWARDS, FELLOW GROWN-UP CHILD STAR BROOKE
SHIELDS, AT A GRAMMYS AFTERPARTY AT JIMMY'S
RESTAURANT IN LOS ANGELES, FEBRUARY 24, 1993.

ABC TV miniseries *The Jacksons: An American Dream,* a sordid but much-watched dramatization of the family's rise from Gary, Indiana to success.

During Black History Month 1992, as part of a goodwill tour, Jackson visited Egypt, Gabon, Ivory Coast, and Tanzania. He spent his time visiting sick children in orphanages and hospitals, but was heavily criticized in the local press for creating unsafe situations as a result of the huge crowds that gathered to see him and for his bizarre behavior, which was often seen as disrespectful.

Questions about Jackson's physical changes continued. In July 1992, he sued the *London Daily Mirror* for slandering him as a "scarred phantom" with a hole in his nose, uneven cheekbones, and a sagging chin. Jackson's lawyers also had to discredit the allegation

that Pepsi had hired a white actor to portray the singer in a commercial.

On February 10, 1993, Jackson decided to give an interview to television superstar Oprah Winfrey. The ninety-minute interview, live on ABC from Neverland Ranch, was designed to confront the mysteries surrounding him. He admitted to having vitiligo—though he does not mention his lupus diagnosis—and in response to accusations that he was a race traitor, Jackson responded, "I'm a Black American . . . I'm proud of my race." He also discredited the hyperbaric oxygen chamber rumor and talked openly about his father's abuse. When Oprah asked if he was a virgin, Jackson cryptically responded that he was a "gentleman" and "You can call me old-fashioned if you want." Ninety million viewers

---

above GREETING A CLASSROOM FULL OF STUDENTS ON HIS 1992 INSIDE AFRICA GOODWILL TOUR.

tuned in and sales of *Dangerous* went through the roof. A few days later, Jackson accepted the Living Legend Award at the Grammys in Los Angeles.

That same month, however, Jackson's scandal quotient reached a disturbing new level. News reports began to surface saying that Los Angeles police were investigating Jackson on child molestation allegations. For years, Jackson had been seen in public with young boys who were sick and terminally ill; he frequently surrounded himself with young celebrity pals like film stars Macaulay Culkin and Corey Haim. It was well known and widely reported in the media—chalked up to Jackson's now legendary eccentricity—that many of these boys stayed at his home or even traveled with him. Jackson had no qualms about telling Oprah, in his February interview, that he regularly surrounded himself with children in an attempt to regain his own lost childhood.

Jackson's relationships with young boys became suspect when, in August 1993, it was announced that Jackson was under investigation by the LAPD on charges that he'd sexually abused Jordan Chandler, a thirteen-year-old boy. Jordan's father, Evan Chandler, a Beverly Hills dentist, had long been suspicious of his son's sleepovers at Neverland. While performing a routine tooth extraction on his son, Evan controversially administered sodium amytal. The so-called "truth serum" barbiturate is known for having inconclusive results, as the subject can be coerced into confirming false memories. Evan claimed that, while drugged, Jordan confessed that he

had been molested by Jackson. Jordan then repeated his confession to a psychiatrist. The abuses were so frequent, Jordan said, that he could provide detailed descriptions of Jackson's unclothed body, including discolored patches on his genitals. The psychiatrist reported these claims to the Department of Children's Services, and, on August 21, 1993, the police searched Neverland, Jackson's other home (a "hideaway" in West Hollywood), and his doctors' offices for evidence.

On September 14, Evan Chandler filed a civil case against Michael Jackson. Jackson's legal team fought back, claiming that the case amounted to nothing more than an extortion attempt. Jackson's sister LaToya spilled her own particular version of the beans in a November interview with Katie Couric, hinting that the accusations were true and that boys might have been paid to keep quiet. Years later, she recanted her story, saying that her abusive husband had forced her to lie.

Extreme stress from the investigation sent Jackson's health spiraling. In Mexico City for a leg of his Dangerous Tour, Jackson released a statement admitting that pain from reconstructive surgery he'd recently had for his 1984 scalp burn had caused him to become addicted to a cocktail of painkillers like Valium, Xanax, and Ativan. He was physically and emotionally exhausted and his weight plummeted. With help from his friend and confidant Elizabeth Taylor, Jackson checked himself into a London drug treatment center on November 12, 1993. The next day, he cancelled the rest of the Dangerous Tour.

opposite PERFORMING IN BUENOS AIRES, ARGENTINA, OCTOBER 12, 1993. THE DANGEROUS TOUR WAS CUT SHORT, JUST ONE MONTH LATER, AFTER ALLEGATIONS SURFACED THAT JACKSON HAD MOLESTED THIRTEEN-YEAR-OLD JORDAN CHANDLER.

MICHAEL
DECEMBER 11, 1993

The Grand
A BALLY'S CASINO RESORT

A PROOF OF A POSTCARD FOR AN EVENT AT A CASINO IN
ATLANTIC CITY, NEW JERSEY. JACKSON WAS UNABLE TO
ATTEND THE EVENT AFTER HE WENT INTO TREATMENT
FOR DRUG DEPENDENCY.

Some fans felt Jackson was being set up by a vindictive LA police department and by a mass media hungry for ratings. Others recoiled at the growing litany of evidence against Jackson. When he returned to the U.S. on December 10 to continue his treatment for drug dependency, his entire family except LaToya came to his defense.

Things got worse. Jackson held a public televised press conference on January 10, 1994, in which he said that he had been "forced to submit to a dehumanizing and humiliating examination by the Santa Barbara County Sheriff's Department and the Los Angeles Police Department earlier this week." He continued, "They served a search warrant on me which allowed them to view and photograph my body, including my penis, my buttocks, my lower torso, thighs, and any other areas that they wanted. They were supposedly looking for any discoloration, spotting, blotches, or other evidence of a skin color disorder called vitiligo which I have previously spoken about." Investigators were indeed looking for evidence to corroborate the young accuser's depiction of Jackson's discolored genitals, in the absence of any witnesses.

On January 16, Jackson threw a party at Neverland for two hundred underprivileged children and invited Black Entertainment Television and KCAL TV to film the event. Kids went before the cameras to protest their host's innocence, though they appeared to be reading from rehearsed scripts.

A week later, on January 25, Jackson settled the civil case out of court for an undisclosed sum, likely around $20 million. Accuser Jordan Chandler, by then fourteen, declined to testify in the criminal case, forcing District Attorney Tom Sneddon to drop it. Because Jackson had not seen the case to trial, where he could have defended himself, many were left with doubts as to his innocence or guilt. Had he bought off his accuser? Whatever the case, this was not the last time Jackson would appear in court on such allegations.

THE KING OF POP AND THE PRINCESS OF ROCK

On May 26, 1994, Jackson shocked the world once again by marrying Elvis's daughter, Lisa Marie Presley, twenty-five. They had known each other slightly for years: Presley first met Jackson in the mid-1970s, when her famous father Elvis took her to see the Jackson 5 on the Las Vegas strip. "She used to come as a little girl and sit right up front . . . She came quite often. And then she'd come backstage and I'd come out and say, 'Hi' and then she'd come again," Jackson recalled in an interview with Diane Sawyer. They reconnected in 1991. According to biographer Randy Taraborrelli, sparks flew at a mutual friend's dinner party. Lisa was attracted to Jackson's edginess and impressed by what Taraborrelli calls "his private candor and normality." They grew closer in the aftermath of the Jordan Chandler allegations, when Presley, herself a recovered drug user, helped counsel the distraught and drug-addicted Jackson. "I wanted to 'save him,'" she said later.

The couple tied the knot in the Dominican Republic province La Vega, near Santo Domingo, and Jackson became stepfather to Presley's two children with musician Danny Keough: two-year-old Danielle and five-year-old Benjamin. Judge Hugo Francisco Alvarez Perez pocketed the tiny sum of fifty-three dollars to run a fifteen-minute private ceremony in his home; he spilled the beans about the nuptials days later to a Santo Domingo daily newspaper. The odd couple denied the marriage at first. It wasn't until August that Lisa Marie issued a press statement to make it official, and Jackson refused to speak openly to the press about the marriage until October. In the lag time, controversy swirled.

Many chalked the union up to one of Jackson's publicity stunts. Tabloid television program *Hard Copy* reported that 87 percent of its audience thought the marriage was a hoax and a *Time*/CNN poll revealed that 41 percent of Americans thought the marriage would last less than a year. Doubters believed that Jackson was trying to rebrand himself as a family man in the wake of his child molestation allegations; aspiring singer Lisa Marie was probably using the marriage to get Jackson to produce her album. Conspiracy theorists went a step further: they painted the marriage as Jackson's shrewd coup to steal Elvis's crown as the King. Jackson already owned the rights to Elvis hits like "Jailhouse Rock" and "Hound Dog" as part of his ATV Music publishing business, and critics had always felt that Neverland was Jackson's attempt to outdo Elvis's palatial Graceland estate. There couldn't have been a better way to be part of the Elvis legacy than to marry his daughter.

Taraborrelli suggests the relationship was genuine, however. He also suggests the couple had an authentic sex life, even though Jackson's neuroses about his physical appearance sometimes got the best of him. Lisa Marie reflected on the relationship on her blog after hearing news of Jackson's death in 2009: "It was an unusual relationship yes, where two unusual people who did not live or know a 'Normal life' found a connection, perhaps with some suspect timing on his part. Nonetheless, I do believe he loved me as much as he could love anyone and I loved him very much."

With the security of knowing that he had his new wife's support and a clean legal record, Jackson began recording a new album in September 1994, full of spite and ready to tell his tale.

above JACKSON AND HIS WIFE, LISA MARIE PRESLEY, VISIT TWO CHILDREN'S HOSPITALS IN BUCHAREST, DISTRIBUTING TOYS TO SICK CHILDREN, ON AUGUST 9, 1994. *opposite* PERFORMING IN BANGKOK, THAILAND ON AUGUST 24, 1993. JACKSON POSTPONED HIS SECOND BANGKOK CONCERT (SCHEDULED FOR THE NEXT DAY), CLAIMING THE CANCELLATION WAS DUE TO DEHYDRATION AND NOT BECAUSE OF THE LA POLICE DEPARTMENT'S INVESTIGATION.

MARRIAGE CERTIFICATE

The marriage certificate making Michael Jackson's May 26, 1994, marriage to Lisa Marie Presley official. Though Jackson's publicists first dismissed the Dominican Republic wedding as a rumor, local newspaper *Listin Diario* ran a photograph of the certificate, which listed the couple's passport numbers.

left JACKSON AND HIS WIFE, LISA MARIE PRESLEY, AT VERSAILLES IN FRANCE O SEPTEMBER 5, 1994. THE NEWLYWEDS FIRST MET IN THE MID-1970S, WHEN LISA MARIE'S FATHER, ELVIS, TOOK HER TO SEE THE JACKSON 5 IN LAS VEGAS. LISA MARIE HELPED MICHAEL RECOVER FROM PRESCRIPTION DRUG ABUSE IN THE WAKE OF THE CHILD MOLESTATION ALLEGATIONS AGAINST HIM IN 1993. *opposite* JACKSON AND LISA MARIE AT THE 1994 MTV VIDEO MUSIC AWARDS.

CHAPTER SEVEN

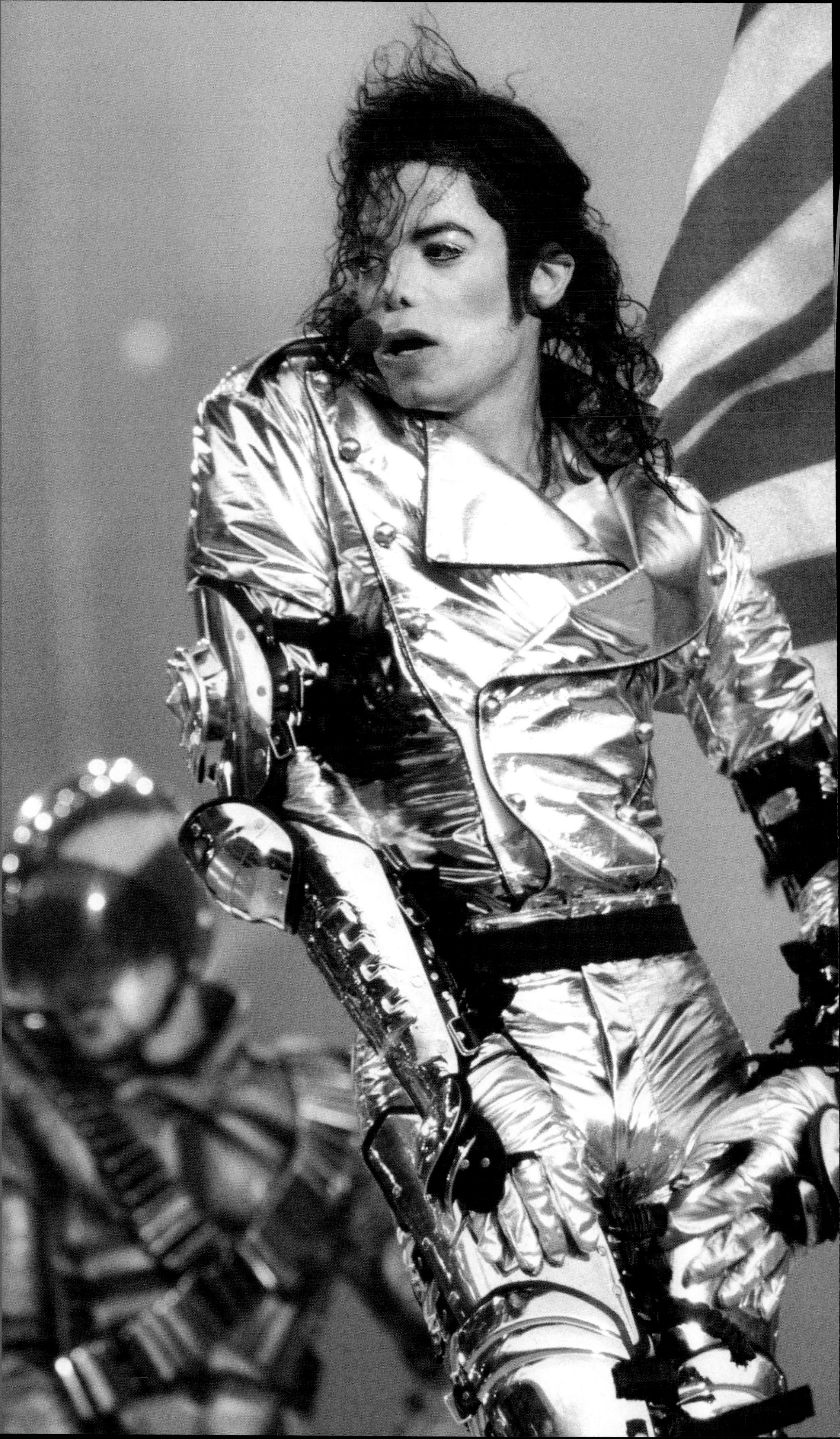

EVERY DAY CREATE YOUR HISTORY

"PERHAPS WHAT MOST SCANDALIZED AMERICA ABOUT THE WHOLE AFFAIR WAS THE DISCOVERY THAT MICHAEL JACKSON WAS A SEXUAL BEING AT ALL."

—Barney Hoskins, writing about Jackson's legal problems in The Independent, *August 1988*

Michael Jackson began 1995 on the offensive, inaugurating his new, Sony/Epic-supported boutique record label, MJJ Music, by introducing the all-female R&B trio Brownstone as his first artists. He later signed his nephews 3T, his sister Maureen (Rebbie), and a small slate of other R&B talent. Also in January, he issued a press statement that he was preemptively instructing his lawyers to sue anyone and everyone slandering his name.

In May 1995, Epic Records launched a $30 million, eighteen-month marketing campaign to generate buzz for Jackson's forthcoming album, *HIStory*. Jackson and his managers, Sandy Gallin and Jim Morey, devised an over-the-top blitz, the most expensive in music history. The centerpiece of the campaign was a four-minute *HIStory* teaser film that played in movie theaters and on television. Shot in Budapest, it featured crowds of weeping prepubescent fans screaming, "We love you, Michael," and parading army troops gathered to watch the revelation of a fifty-foot Soviet-style statue of the pop star.

opposite ON TOUR IN SUPPORT OF HIS NEW ALBUM, *HISTORY*, JACKSON PERFORMS AT LONDON'S WEMBLEY STADIUM.

is a perfunctory greatest-hits package, and disc two is a collection of fourteen new recordings plus a hard rock cover of the Beatles's "Come Together" recorded for the 1989 *Moonwalker* film. The confessional album finds Jackson bluntly condemning the forces he saw as threats. His principal targets were mostly personal—tabloid magazines and the Los Angeles district attorney's office—but he was also after global targets like social injustice, intolerance, and environmental destruction.

Despite the self-importance, there are some musical gems. Jackson wrote, produced, and played instruments on twelve of the album's fifteen new recordings, and he also performed a grandiose orchestral cover of what he called his favorite song, the Charlie Chaplin song "Smile," which talks about putting on a happy face to mask one's internal pain. Critics seemed to gloss over some of the more subtle beauties of the album: "Stranger in Moscow" is forlorn, plaintive, gossamer—Jackson at his most stripped down.

This clip was widely considered the most astonishing and megalomaniacal promotional video of all time. To drive the point home, nine of those fifty-foot steel and fiberglass statues were erected in different countries in Europe, and one was floated down the River Thames. Jackson wanted the world to know he was still the King of Pop, and he was willing to go to outrageous lengths to prove it. The *HIStory* teaser, with its overblown religious and political iconography, suggested that Jackson had developed a serious savior complex. The classic indicators were all present: grandiose fantasies of self-importance, excessive need for approval, rage, social isolation, and depression. Jackson had clearly lost all sense of proportion and scale.

The 150-minute double disc, *HIStory: Past, Present, Future, Book 1,* was released on June 3, 1995. Disc one

In the blistering debut single, "Scream," Jackson shared a duet with sister Janet. It topped the Beatles' "Let It Be" as the highest first-week showing for any single in history. Co-produced by Janet's longtime collaborators, Jimmy Jam and Terry Lewis, "Scream" is a cacophony of crashing guitars, buzzing synthesizers, and drill-like techno beats. An irate Michael and Janet order their persecutors: "Stop pressuring me / It makes me want to scream." The video portrayed the siblings as exiles cruising around in a luxury black-and-white spacecraft.

above JACKSON REACHES OUT A HAND AT A CONCERT IN NEW YORK CITY. *opposite* A FIFTY-FOOT STATUE OF MICHAEL JACKSON FLOATING DOWN THE THAMES IN LONDON. IT WAS ONE OF NINE IDENTICAL STATUES DISTRIBUTED ACROSS EUROPE TO PROMOTE *HISTORY*.

however, barely seemed appropriate for such a heartwarming tune: a short-haired, skinny, and pale Jackson cavorted around in the nude with Lisa Marie; the couple concealed their private parts with strategically-placed towels. "They Don't Care About Us," a spare, singsong chant set over ethnic beats featured the unlikely combination of guitarist Slash of Guns N' Roses and the Andrae Crouch Gospel Choir; its Spike Lee–directed video was shot in the favelas of Brazil and showcased the percussion group Olodum. When criticized by Jewish groups for using an anti-Semitic slur in the lyrics, Jackson pulled the album and re-released it on his own dime. Fifteen million units later, *HIStory* emerged as the bestselling double album of all time.

It picked up eleven nominations and three awards at the MTV Video Music Awards. Budgeted at $7 million, it secured a place in the *Guinness Book of World Records* for the most expensive video ever.

To promote *HIStory,* Jackson and Lisa Marie gave their first joint, live interview on June 14 to ABC TV's "Prime Time Live." Sixty million viewers tuned in to watch host Diane Sawyer question Jackson and Lisa Marie—albeit gently—about the authenticity of their marriage. "We have a normal house," Lisa Marie protests. "We have a nanny, we have a maid and we walk around and he's . . . in the studio, I'm in the kitchen. We're running around like normal." Many found the entire affair awkward, contrived, and unconvincing.

Other songs on *HIStory* kept Jackson in the news. His inspirational ballad "You Are Not Alone," written and co-produced by R. Kelly, debuted in August on the Hot 100 at number one, the first song ever to enter that chart in the top spot. The Wayne Isham-directed video,

In November, Japanese corporation Sony offered Jackson $90 million for 50 percent of the ATV Music Publishing company he'd purchased in 1985, and Jackson accepted. The lucrative move meant that he had essentially doubled his original investment. The new venture, Sony/ATV Publishing, became one of the world's largest music publishers, owning the rights to more than 400,000 songs—everyone from Mariah Carey to Bob Dylan to the Beatles. Some speculated that Jackson sold his share out of necessity, to support his lavish lifestyle at Neverland and the inflated promotional budgets for his album releases. "This acquisition had nothing to do with needing funds," Jackson retorted in *USA Today*. "It's just a great move, a corporate, entrepreneurial thing to do. It's smart business. It's about growth. Everything in life to me is about growth."

above RIDING THE BUMPER CARS AT NEVERLAND, HIS RETREAT FROM THE WORLD. *opposite (above)* DANCING ON THE ROOF OF A BUILDING IN THE DONA MARTA SLUM OF RIO DE JANEIRO, BRAZIL, DURING THE FILMING OF THE VIDEO FOR "THEY DON'T CARE ABOUT US." *BILLBOARD* MAGAZINE CREDITED JACKSON FOR HELPING TO KICKSTART ECONOMIC IMPROVEMENT IN THE SLUM. *opposite (below)* ON THE SET OF THE VIDEO FOR "THEY DON'T CARE ABOUT US."

ANOTHER TURN

In December 1995, Jackson's health took a turn for the worse. He collapsed while rehearsing for an HBO special and was taken to Beth Israel Medical Center North in New York. The doctors chalked up the problem to virus-related dehydration that had affected his heart, liver, and kidneys. Famous family and friends—Lisa Marie, mother Katherine, sister Janet, Diana Ross—came to visit him during the highly publicized hospital stay. The workaholic star was ordered to take a one-month vacation, and his friend and business associate Prince Al-Waleed bin Talal bin Abdulaziz al-Saud of Saudi Arabia, one of the world's richest men, whisked him off to France to visit Euro Disney.

Reports had begun to circulate that Jackson was separated from Lisa Marie. Biographer Taraborrelli claims

that Jackson had become obsessed with the idea of having children. Lisa Marie, on the other hand, felt Jackson was too emotionally immature to make such a commitment. He was angry, but, as Tarraborrelli puts it, "she had no patience at all with the lost childhood routine. 'Who hasn't had a miserable childhood?' she would say." She claims the relationship had long been over, and that having a child would just lead to a custody battle later.

When Jackson threateningly suggested that his friend Debbie Rowe—a woman he'd met while she was a nurse working for his dermatologist, Arnie Klein—would be willing to produce children on his behalf, Lisa reportedly called his bluff and stormed out of the relationship. She later claimed in her blog, "I became very ill and emotionally/spiritually exhausted in my quest to save him from certain self-destructive behavior and

above IN MUMBAI, INDIA, ON THE HISTORY WORLD TOUR. *opposite* JACKSON WOWS THE CROWD AT THE MTV VIDEO MUSIC AWARDS AT RADIO CITY MUSIC HALL, NEW YORK CITY, IN SEPTEMBER 1995. HIS FIFTEEN-MINUTE GREATEST-HITS MEDLEY INCLUDED THREE COSTUME CHANGES.

TICKET

A January 1997 ticket from the HIStory World Tour. Michael Jackson performed two sold-out nights at Aloha Stadium in Hawaii—his first U.S. appearance since 1989.

BACKSTAGE PASS

A special backstage pass sticker from the HIStory World Tour, which kicked off in 1996 and focused on Europe, Africa, Asia, and Australia. It was Michael Jackson's first solo concert tour not sponsored by Pepsi, and it would be the last tour of his career.

left ON STAGE IN NEW YORK CITY DURING THE U.S. LEG OF THE HISTORY WORLD TOUR. *opposite* IN BREMEN, GERMANY, DURING THE EUROPEAN LEG OF THE TOUR IN 1997.

from the awful vampires and leeches he would always manage to magnetize around him." In January 1996, after eighteen months of marriage, Lisa Marie filed for divorce, citing irreconcilable differences. It became final in August of that year.

When Jackson performed at the BRIT Awards in February 1996, he sang the third single from *HIStory*, environmentalist ballad "Earth Song," surrounded by a cast of children in tattered clothes and a rabbi. In the middle of the performance, Jarvis Cocker, lead singer of rock band Pulp, interrupted the solemn performance by running on stage and shaking his behind at the audience. Jackson was enraged.

Cocker claimed he was protesting Michael Jackson: "My actions were a form of protest at the way Michael Jackson sees himself as some kind of Christ-like figure with the power of healing. The music industry allows him to indulge his fantasies because of his wealth and power. People go along with it even though they know it's a bit sick. I just couldn't go along with it anymore."

Then a strange thing happened in the media. Letters of support for Cocker's bizarre actions started pouring in from fans and even celebrities. Cocker was clearly not the only one who thought Jackson was drowning in narcissism. Ironically, though, Cocker's protest helped to boost *HIStory* sales.

Jackson spent much of the rest of 1996 preparing for the HIStory World Tour, a massive special effects–laden show that started with a spaceship crashing out of the stage floor. The tour kicked off September 7, 1996, in Prague. It broke attendance records all over Europe and in Asia. At thirty-nine, as journalist Paul Lester wrote in *Uncut*, Jackson had become the oldest artist in music history to elicit pre-teen mass hysteria.

above JACKSON'S FOOTWEAR FOR HIS VARIOUS COSTUME CHANGES BACKSTAGE IN BREMEN, GERMANY. *opposite (above)* JACKSON STRIKES A BEATIFIC POSE, SURROUNDED BY CHILDREN AT THE BRIT AWARDS ON FEBRUARY 19, 1996. *opposite (below)* ON STAGE AT THE BRIT AWARDS, WHERE ROCK SINGER JARVIS COCKER PROTESTED WHAT HE SAW AS JACKSON'S NARCISSISM.

CHAPTER EIGHT

THE VINCIBLE KING OF POP

"WELL, I USUALLY AM HAPPY. I DON'T LET ANYTHING GET ME DOWN, NO MATTER WHAT. I LIKE TO HEAR THE SOUND OF WATER AND BIRDS CHIRPING AND LAUGHTER, YOU KNOW. I LOVE ALL THE REAL NATURAL, INNOCENT THINGS."

–Michael Jackson, when asked if he is happy, in TV Guide, *December 1999*

On November 14, 1996, in Sydney, Australia, Michael Jackson and Debbie Rowe, a "hard-talking, hard-drinking, Harley Davidson-riding" nurse who worked for Jackson's dermatologist, were married in a small ceremony. Three months later, on February 13, 1997, Rowe gave birth to Jackson's first son, Prince Michael Jackson Junior. The child's unlikely godparents were the film stars Elizabeth Taylor and Macaulay Culkin.

His busy schedule hardly let up after his son's birth. In May, the Jackson 5 were inducted into the Rock and Roll Hall of Fame, and Diana Ross served as the presenter. That same month, Jackson released *Blood on the Dance Floor: HIStory in the Mix*, a club-oriented dance album containing remixes of eight songs from *HIStory*, along with five original songs. Lead single "Blood on the Dance Floor," co-written and co-produced with Teddy Riley, sank like a stone on the charts, peaking at number

opposite DURING AN INTERVIEW WITH BARBARA WALTERS AT A HOTEL IN PARIS FOR ABC'S *20/20* ON SEPTEMBER 7, 1997, A FEW MONTHS AFTER THE BIRTH OF HIS FIRST CHILD, PRINCE MICHAEL.

that Jackson and Rowe entered into a legally binding agreement on January 23, 1996. Rowe was artificially inseminated on May 28 and 29, 1996. Four months after Prince was born, Rowe was inseminated again. In both cases, the sperm was anonymously donated; Jackson was most likely not the biological father. Jackson and Rowe announced their divorce in October 1999, after only three years of marriage. According to court documents, she received as part of the settlement a $2 million Beverly Hills home, a one-off sum of $4 or $5 million, and an annual payment of $900,000. She eventually gave up all visitation rights and agreed to remain bound by a confidentiality agreement.

forty-two. In the first month of its release, the album sold a paltry 79,000 copies. But *Blood on the Dance Floor,* in many ways, should have been a reminder that Jackson's core audience had long since left the U.S. The original intention of the release was to add a spark to his European summer tour, and *Blood on the Dance Floor* did top the radio airplay and album charts in Europe.

In April 1998, Debbie Rowe gave birth to a second child, a girl named Paris Michael Katherine. When a reporter asked Jackson about rumors that Rowe was a surrogate, rather than the biological mother of the children, Jackson responded that the story was "total garbage. It's just trash and not true." The singer continued to insist that he was the biological father of Paris and Prince Michael, though in photos the children appeared to be very light-skinned and did not look like him. What we know now to be true, thanks to legal documents filed by Rowe herself in 2004, is

Regardless of the curious way he organized his domestic life, Jackson's artistic reputation remained strong. In April 2001, Jackson was inducted into the Rock and Roll Hall of Fame as a solo artist. That fall, Jackson was feted at a special concert at Madison Square Garden, *Michael Jackson: 30th Anniversary Celebration, The Solo Years.* The live celebrations occurred September 7 and September 10, and CBS broadcast the concert in November. Viewers numbering 25.7 million watched as a slew of top performers, including Whitney Houston, Luther Vandross, Liza Minnelli, and Usher paid tribute to Jackson. He attended with his parents, Elizabeth Taylor,

directional A LIMITED EDITION AMSTERDAM ARENA PROMOTIONAL CARD FOR MICHAEL JACKSON'S 1997 ALBUM *BLOOD ON THE DANCE FLOOR.* THE ALBUM FAILED MISERABLY IN THE UNITED STATES, BUT WAS A MAJOR HIT OVERSEAS. MANY EUROPEAN FANS SENT IN SCATHING LETTERS TO AMERICAN MUSIC JOURNALISTS, WHO SAVAGED THE RECORD IN THE PRESS.

ON THE FIRST NIGHT OF THE CONCERT *MICHAEL JACKSON: 30TH ANNIVERSARY CELEBRATION, THE SOLO YEARS*, SEPTEMBER 7 AT MADISON SQUARE GARDEN.

MICHAEL JACKSON AT THE FIRST SIGNING EVENT IN
SUPPORT OF HIS 2001 ALBUM, *INVINCIBLE*. THE ALBUM
DEBUTED AT NUMBER ONE ON THE *BILLBOARD* CHARTS.

and Macaulay Culkin. Jackson reunited for the first time in twenty years with his brothers for a greatest-hits medley, and then performed his own solo set.

INVINCIBLE

That same month, Jackson released his tenth studio album, *Invincible*, a strong, if not cohesive, collection of new recordings. A number of the songs were co-produced by R&B wunderkind Rodney Jerkins, who brought the same tight-pocket digital grooves and fondness for melody that he'd previously delivered to artists like Destiny's Child and Brandy. Debut single "You Rock My World" was a sleek, lean slab of piano techno-funk that rose to number ten on the charts. The Grammy-nominated $5 million video co-starred Marlon Brando and Chris Tucker. *Invincible* debuted at number one and went double platinum. Sales, however, were markedly lower than any previous Michael Jackson album; it vanished from the album charts within a month.

In response to the September 11 terrorist attacks on New York City and Washington DC, Jackson put together an impromptu celebrity charity concert in November called *United We Stand: What More Can I Give*, titled after one of the singles from *Invincible*.

The single "What More Can I Give," however, was never distributed because a war was brewing between Jackson and his longtime label. Jackson claimed that Sony was deliberately sabotaging his projects in the attempt to bankrupt him and steal back his 50 percent share of Sony/ATV Publishing. In July, Jackson joined

Reverend Al Sharpton for a televised rally to campaign for recording artists' rights and accused the head of Sony, Tony Mottola, of racism. "If you fight for me, you're fighting for all black people, dead and alive," Jackson said. Clearly, the pop star's persecution complex had grown, rather than waned; Sharpton distanced himself from Jackson in the immediate aftermath of the event. At the same time, many of the points Jackson raised about the need for recording artists to fight for better rights from record labels had some validity. Sadly, the good work he could have done for other artists was hampered by the self-serving impression he gave.

NEW REVELATIONS

In September 2002, it became public news that Jackson had fathered a third child with an unnamed mother, a boy named Prince Michael II. Jackson nicknamed him Blanket. Scandal once again ensued when Jackson, staying in Berlin to receive a humanitarian award,

above JACKSON AND HIS WIFE, DEBBIE ROWE, WAVE TO FANS FROM THE BALCONY OF THE HOTEL ROYAL MONCEAU IN PARIS, 1997.

NOTEPAD PAGE

A piece of decorative notepad paper
from Neverland Ranch. The emblem of
a boy sitting on a crescent moon was
emblazoned on many of the household items
at Neverland, including soaps. Jackson's
uncontained penchant for fantasy and
childhood would be both a blessing and a
curse in his rollercoaster career.

CERTIFICATE

Michael had a working narrow-gauge railroad
built on the sprawling Neverland Ranch
property in 1992. The steam train, named
Katherine after his mother, had 24-karat
gold-leaf lettering and a state-of-the-art
stereo system.

left TAPING A PERFORMANCE FOR
AMERICAN BANDSTAND'S 50TH
ANNIVERSARY CELEBRATION IN 2002.
opposite MICHAEL JACKSON, A LIFELONG
ANIMAL LOVER, HOLDS A KOALA
IN SYDNEY ON A BREAK FROM HIS
AUSTRALIAN TOUR IN MAY 1998.

momentarily held Blanket—who had a cloth over his face—over a hotel balcony, presumably attempting to show him to the public. It was an incredibly dangerous move, and the press moved quickly to condemn Jackson as the world's worst father. The video was repeated on news broadcasts all over the world. "I made a terrible mistake," Jackson said in a public statement. "I got caught up in the excitement of the moment. I would never intentionally endanger the lives of my children."

Later that year, acting on a suggestion from his friend, the magician Uri Geller, Jackson agreed to appear in a Granada Television documentary hosted by British journalist Martin Bashir. The concept was that Jackson would be filmed over the course of eight months so he could finally give the public an authentic glimpse into his private life. This would be a television coup, given Jackson's enigmatic, obsessively guarded lifestyle.

Things went south very fast. The documentary, which aired in the United Kingdom and the United States in early February 2003, shows Bashir grilling Jackson on a number of points, including the issue of plastic surgery. Bashir was accused of deliberately attempting to distort Jackson's image for the sake of ratings, but it can also be said that Jackson gave him plenty of material. Jackson lies repeatedly throughout the interview, particularly in his claims that he has only had minor surgery. He says at first that Blanket was conceived naturally, but admits later that he hired a surrogate mother. His children make brief appearances

on film, covered in veils and masks—purportedly to protect them from kidnapping attempts. Jackson himself appears frail and disheveled on screen. His pale face looks artificial, unshaven and yet feminine.

Jackson's delusional, out-of-touch state is confirmed when he takes Bashir on a shopping spree and spends over $1 million on trinkets and furniture. Given the tenuous state of Jackson's finances at the time—court documents show he owed more than $400 million in unpaid loans— the spree seems conspicuously staged.

The program becomes most controversial when Jackson defends his admission that he still sleeps in the same bedroom as the teenage boys he invites over to his ranch. Most disturbingly, Jackson is filmed holding hands with his "special friend" Gavin Arvizo, a thirteen-year-old recovering cancer patient. The boy, who says he considers Jackson "his best friend," rests his head on Jackson's shoulder.

Outrage ensued when the documentary was aired. Jackson, feeling Bashir had conspired to paint a negative portrait, hired his own film crew to produce and distribute a rebuttal video in which Arvizo, his brother, and his mother supposedly praise the singer. Matters got more complicated when Arvizo's family claimed that Jackson and his henchmen attempted to hold them at the Neverland Ranch against their will to control the negative PR created by Bashir's documentary. In the aftermath, Gavin's mother, Janet Arvizo, visited the same lawyer and psychiatrist who had represented Evan

opposite (above) A COURTROOM DRAWING SHOWING JACKSON WITH HIS NEW LAWYER, THOMAS MESEREAU, DURING THE HEARING WHERE JACKSON PLEADED NOT GUILTY TO MOLESTING GAVIN ARVIZO. *opposite (below)* LEAVING THE SANTA BARBARA COUNTY COURTHOUSE AFTER HEARING THE INSTRUCTIONS GIVEN TO THE JURY, JUNE 1, 2005.

Chandler in the earlier case, even before going to the police. Gavin's brother, Star, claimed to have witnessed the abuse.

On November 20, 2003, Jackson surrendered himself to the police after being indicted on four counts of molesting a minor, four counts of intoxicating a minor, one count of abduction, and one count of conspiring to hold the boy and his family captive. He was handcuffed and taken to the Santa Barbara County Jail with his head hanging low. This was the lowest moment yet in his career.

Jackson pulled many strange, possibly drug-fueled stunts throughout the four months of the trial, including wearing his pajamas to court and woozily being carried into the courtroom by his bodyguards. But Jackson's carefully constructed veils of enigma and eccentricity seemed to crumble away like dust as the trial wore on. He could do nothing to match the parade of lurid information that spilled out during the various testimonies. The public learned about his back and neck pain, and the array of prescription drugs he had started abusing again; they learned about his spending problem, his drinking problem, and his pornography collection. It also came out that he had settled a case in the late '80s with his maid: her seven-year-old son claimed that Jackson had fondled him and Jackson paid the family $2 million to keep it out of the courts.

Despite the salacious revelations, the prosecution's case was riddled with problems. The timeline of events that they proposed seemed unlikely, and they relied on

dubious testimony from numerous disgruntled employees of Neverland. The accuser's mother, Janet Arvizo, who had previously lied under oath in an unrelated case, was by turns a hostile and discombobulated witness. Only one boy who claimed to have been victimized would testify, while other boys with whom Jackson had associated, including Macaulay Culkin, praised Jackson and said they had never been abused in any way.

The prosecution called Debbie Rowe to testify against her ex-husband, assuming she had an ax to grind. But shockingly, Rowe had only positive things to say about Jackson. By all accounts, she had deliberately manipulated the prosecution into believing she was on their side. The prosecution had lost its ace in the hole.

On June 13, 2005, the jury reached a verdict of not guilty on all counts.

---

above A GROUP OF FANS FROM PARIS, FRANCE, GATHER OUTSIDE NEVERLAND TO READ THE *SANTA MARIA TIMES*' ACCOUNT OF JACKSON'S ACQUITTAL. *opposite* JACKSON ARRIVES AT THE COURTHOUSE ON APRIL 30, 2004.

CHAPTER NINE

LAST DAYS

"A LOT OF ENTERTAINERS, THEY MAKE MONEY AND THEY SPEND THE REST OF THEIR LIFE CELEBRATING THAT ONE GOAL THEY REACHED . . . AND THEN THEY TRY TO STRAIGHTEN UP AND THEY SAY 'WHO AM I? WHERE AM I? WHAT HAPPENED?' AND THEY LOST THEMSELVES, AND THEY'RE BROKEN. YOU HAVE TO BE CAREFUL AND HAVE SOME KIND OF DISCIPLINE."

–*Michael Jackson in* Creem *magazine, June 1983*

While fans outside the courthouse applauded and cried and hugged, and while his mother cried for joy behind him in the stands, Jackson sat motionless. Though the charges and the long trial were behind him, Jackson could not be free. People could now see through all of his masks. The public had seen another side of Neverland, the slow descent from dream to nightmare. Most of what they saw was chaotic, reckless, and decadent, but some elements, like the porn magazines in the bathroom and the stacks of unpaid bills, just seemed mundane and sad. Jackson could hardly play the savior on high now.

opposite MICHAEL JACKSON'S STAR ON THE HOLLYWOOD WALK OF FAME.

After the trial, Jackson left with his children to Bahrain to stay with Sheik Abdulla bin Hamad Al Khalifa, the second son of the King of Bahrain. Journalists reported that financial problems would force Jackson to close the main house on Neverland Ranch. In response, he formed a company called Colony Capital, LLC through which he retained part ownership of Neverland. He refinanced his stake in the Sony/ATV catalog; he was still earning $75 million a year just from royalties. But with multi-million-dollar loans coming due, how long could he hold onto this prized asset?

THE COMEBACK

In 2008, Michael issued *Thriller 25*, an updated packaging of his masterwork. The release signaled the beginning of

an attempt to re-crown himself as the King of Pop. In 2008, Randy Phillips of AEG Live, an event company, announced he was in talks with Michael Jackson and Jackson tour manager Paul Gongaware. Jackson stood to make a badly needed $100 million from This is It, a concert residency series at London's O2 arena beginning in summer 2009. It would be a spectacular extravaganza—right up Jackson's alley. Swarovski Crystals announced that it would provide 300,000 pieces of crystal to wash the stage in glitter. Jackson would perform twenty-seven shows between July and September, receive a three-month break, and perform another twenty-three shows between January and March 2010.

On March 5, 2009, Michael held a press conference: as he had with all of his previous solo tours, he announced it as his "final curtain call," the last chance to see him. The tickets sold out in a single morning. After all he had been through, Jackson could still sell one million tickets in a matter of hours. R&B singer Akon, with whom Jackson was cutting a new album, told the *Washington Post*, "His kids are like his first priority, and they had never seen him perform live. He was trying to create the most incredible show for his kids."

He appeared to be excited about the idea of getting back on stage, and was happy to be working with his old manager Frank Dileo again. "The show at the Staples Center was amazing," Dileo told the *Hollywood Reporter*. "Michael rehearsed ten or eleven songs. He sang and danced, not always at full power, but the way you do for

above VISITING THE TROOPS AT THE U.S. ARMY BASE IN JAPAN, CAMP ZAMA, ON MARCH 10, 2007.

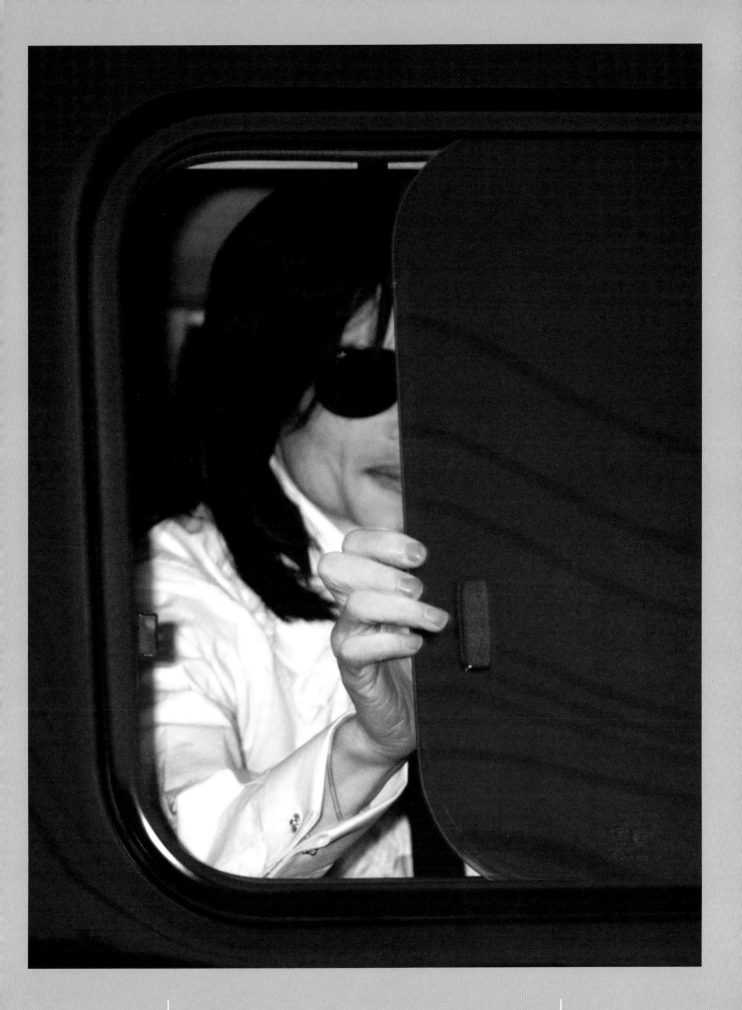

FORTY-EIGHT-YEAR-OLD MICHAEL JACKSON ATTENDS A
$3,500-A-TICKET "PREMIUM VIP PARTY" IN TOKYO ON MARCH
8, 2007. MICHAEL MAINTAINED A HUGE FAN BASE IN TOKYO;
SCREAMING CROWDS GREETED HIM AT THE AIRPORT.

COURT DOCUMENT

On June 13, 2005, Michael Jackson was acquitted on all charges related to his criminal trial in Santa Maria, California, including charges of child abduction, false imprisonment, and molestation. Fans waiting outside the courtroom cheered and sobbed uncontrollably in joy and relief.

WILL

A copy of Michael Jackson's 2002 will. Jackson's lawyer, John Branca, read the will at Jermaine Jackson's house. Their mother, Katherine Jackson, was named guardian of Michael Jackson's three children and beneficiary of 40 percent of his estate.

TICKET

On July 7, 2009, an official star-studded memorial service to honor the memory of Michael Jackson was held at the Staples Center in Los Angeles. Tickets were given away via an online lottery: 1.6 million people applied for only 8,750 tickets that were open to the public. In the end, 11,000 people filled the Staples Center and 6,500 were seated in the adjacent Nokia Theatre. Between 5,000 and 15,000 fans without tickets waited outside the venue.

left AT THE 2009 PRESS CONFERENCE
ANNOUNCING THE O2 ARENA CONCERTS.
opposite SILHOUETTED AT THE CONCERT
*MICHAEL JACKSON, 30TH ANNIVERSARY
CELEBRATION, THE SOLO YEARS.*

a run-through. When the show was over, he called me, but I was in the back getting something. He found me, and said, 'Frank, I am so happy.' He said he was just so happy. He said, 'This is really our time.' He put his arm around me."

Jackson was very much involved in putting the show together. A perfectionist, he wanted to be involved with many of the details. He was listening to sound levels, checking mixes, and helping to select backup dancers. He was training with Lou Ferrigno, the actor who once played the Incredible Hulk, trying to get back into shape. Kenny Ortega, the director of the This Is It concert series, saw how Jackson was developing. "There was this one moment," he recalled to the *Associated Press*, "he was moving across the stage and he was doing these trademark Michael moves, and I know I got this big grin on my face, and I started thinking to myself, 'You know, it's been years since I've seen that.'"

Jackson was enjoying the process of developing the stage show for This Is It and was excited to be back on stage, but by all accounts, he was in no shape to perform. He was hooked on Demerol, morphine, and a cocktail of other prescription drugs and sedatives. He had a motley crew of sycophants supporting his addictive, self-destructive behavior. Jackson had asked AEG Live to put his physician, cardiologist Conrad Murray, on the payroll. And so he was—at $150,000 a month.

Jackson was 5'10"—people were always surprised that he was that tall—and he weighed only 126 pounds. He was gaunt and pale at the age of fifty. But he really had made himself ageless. He looked like he was not of this world. His long black hair descended down over his ears to his shoulders. His jaw had become completely square, his lips brightly rouged.

On June 25, he died of cardiac arrest.

---

opposite AT A PRESS CONFERENCE AT THE LONDON O2 ARENA ON MARCH 5, 2009, JACKSON ANNOUNCED THIS IS IT, A SERIES OF FIFTY CONCERTS THAT HE CLAIMED WOULD BE HIS "FINAL CURTAIN CALL," HIS LAST LIVE PERFORMANCES EVER. HE HAD NOT TOURED IN TWELVE YEARS. *above* NINETEEN-YEAR-OLD FAN AYESHA OBI OF LONDON COLLECTS THE FIRST TICKET FOR JACKSON'S SERIES OF CONCERTS AT THE O2 ARENA ON MARCH 13, 2009.

AFTERWORD: WRESTLING WITH MEMORIES

THE NIGHT BEFORE MICHAEL JACKSON DIED, HE WAS IN REHEARSALS

at the booming, empty Staples Center in downtown Los Angeles, doing what he did best. When he collapsed at home the next day, his physician was there.

Jackson's longtime obsessions with health and medical procedures had come to haunt him. For almost two years, it appears that Jackson received Propofol, a powerful sedative used in hospital surgeries under careful monitoring, in order to fight insomnia. News reports claim Jackson was administered Propofol in the twenty-four hours before his death.

Dr. Conrad Murray, Jackson's private physician, was staying at Holmby Hills. On the morning of June 25, he claims he found the singer in his bedroom, unconscious. Murray put one hand under Jackson's back and pushed down on his chest with the other. When paramedics arrived they spent another forty-five minutes trying to

above A STATUE OF MICHAEL JACKSON, MUCH LIKE THE *HISTORY* PROMOTIONAL STATUES, IN REGENSDORF, SWITZERLAND, NEAR ZURICH. THE NEARLY-FORTY-FOOT STATUE WAS DISPLAYED AFTER HIS DEATH FROM JULY 3 TO JULY 5, 2009. *opposite* JACKSON TOSSES HIS TRADEMARK FEDORA WHILE DANCING ON STAGE. FRED ASTAIRE ONCE CALLED HIM "ONE HELL OF A MOVER."

A FEDORA, SUNGLASSES, AND A SINGLE WHITE GLOVE
ON STAGE AT HARLEM'S APOLLO THEATER BESIDE A
LONE MICROPHONE, BEFORE THE PUBLIC MEMORIAL FOR
THE KING OF POP ON JUNE 30, 2009.

revive Jackson before taking him to UCLA Medical Center. Huge crowds gathered outside the hospital before the doctors pronounced him dead.

When the news broke, it was like a seismic shock around the world. The energy rippled out, gushed out, everywhere at once, spontaneously, unscripted, from the heart.

Outside the tall glass doors of the Apollo Theater on 125th Street in Harlem—that famous theater where Joe first brought the boys in 1967 for Amateur Night, their lucky break—people were doing the moonwalk,

jumping and shouting and singing "Billie Jean" and "Wanna Be Startin' Somethin'."

On street corners everywhere you went, there was a radio blasting a song that you loved—"Remember the Time," "Billie Jean," "Dancing Machine"—or a Michael Jackson song you hadn't heard in a long time. "Stranger in Moscow," maybe, or "Another Part of Me."

And there was a sense that day that what you were feeling was being felt all the way around the world at the same time. In China, every headline let you know that Michael Jackson was "the most outstanding singer

above MICHAEL JACKSON FANS GATHER OUTSIDE THE NOTRE DAME CATHEDRAL IN PARIS, FRANCE, ON JUNE 26, 2009, THE DAY AFTER JACKSON'S DEATH. THE MASSIVE GLOBAL OUTPOURING OF GRIEF DEMONSTRATED THAT, WHILE THE PRESS HAD FOCUSED ALMOST EXCLUSIVELY ON THE CONTROVERSIAL ASPECTS OF JACKSON'S CAREER, HIS CORE FANS HAD LONG AGO ACCEPTED THE SINGER'S ECCENTRICITIES AS PART AND PARCEL OF HIS UNDENIABLE TALENT.

biggest show of all time, on the biggest stage. It was the most magical vanishing act ever. But this really would be his last show.

There will never be another Michael Jackson. He merged so many artistic traditions together: Broadway, soul, rock, easy listening, glam rock, breakdancing, and so much more. He learned from the greats, like James Brown and Sammy Davis Jr., and was supported by great record labels, Motown and Epic, at the height of their brilliance and financial power. Most young pop artists owe Michael a huge debt, and they haven't been shy to admit it. Michael is there in the slick moves of Chris Brown and Usher and in the razzle-dazzle of pop acts like Justin Timberlake and Britney Spears. And music fans continue to look for performers who sing and dance with the same energetic abandon, the same obsessive attention to detail, the same unwillingness to settle for mediocrity.

of all time." In Rio de Janeiro, Governor Sergio Cabral planned to erect a Michael Jackson statue in the Dona Marta slum where Jackson had filmed the video for "They Don't Really Care About Us." In Victoria, British Columbia, a dance troupe called Atomic Vaudeville took to the downtown streets in a flash-mob performance of the choreography from Jackson's *Thriller* video. Fans gathered spontaneously in Mexico City at the Angel of Independence monument, and at the gates of the U.S. Embassy in Moscow and in Tokyo's Yoyogi Park. His songs shot to the top of the iTunes popularity rankings—Michael was back on top of the charts.

Few public figures could ever elicit that type of response. In death, Michael finally got his wish for the

To honor Michael Jackson, you have to celebrate the whole human being—the things that made him human, and the things that made him seem otherworldly. When I think about his story, I think of the tragedy and the triumph, the narcissism and the selflessness, the isolation and the fame, the shyness and the shrewdness, the schmaltz and the soul, the freakshow and the confessional. He was all of that at the same time.

There are few souls who can light up the entire world with that degree of intensity, only a precious few who ever shine that brilliantly. May he thrill us forever.

---

above JACKSON'S FAMILY GATHERED AT THE PUBLIC MEMORIAL SERVICE ON JULY 7, 2009, AT THE STAPLES CENTER IN LOS ANGELES. FROM LEFT: JACKSON'S SISTER LATOYA WITH HIS CHILDREN PARIS MICHAEL KATHERINE, ELEVEN, PRINCE MICHAEL II, SEVEN, AND PRINCE MICHAEL, TWELVE. *opposite* JACKSON ON STAGE AT LONDON'S WEMBLEY STADIUM IN 1988, WHEN HE SET THE WORLD RECORD FOR THE MOST SUCCESSFUL CONCERT SERIES OF ALL TIME.

ABOUT THE AUTHOR

Jason King, Ph.D., is Artistic Director and Associate Professor of the Clive Davis Department of Recorded Music, an innovative undergraduate training program for creative music entrepreneurs at Tisch School of the Arts, New York University that he helped launch. His articles on R&B, hip-hop, and pop have appeared in numerous anthologies and magazines, including *Vibe*, the *Village Voice*, and *Blender*. He has given lectures on popular music at universities such as Harvard, Princeton, Stanford, Yale, and Columbia. Jason's book *Blue Magic*, which looks at the mechanics of energy and spirit in contemporary popular music, is forthcoming from Duke University Press. Jason also works as producer, musical supervisor, songwriter, live event producer, music manager, and marketing and branding consultant for a wide variety of record labels and recording artists. He hails from Canada.

ACKNOWLEDGMENTS

Thanks to family and friends for the support; to Kristin and Kjersti for the guidance in bringing this to completion; and to Ann Powers for the opportunity.

IMAGE CREDITS

Every effort has been made to trace copyright holders. If any unintentional omissions have been made, becker&mayer! would be pleased to add appropriate acknowledgments in future editions.

Front cover: Kevin Mazur/WireImage
Title page: Larry Busacca/WireImage
Contents page: Time Life Pictures/DMI/Getty Images
Page 6: Michael Ochs Archives/Getty Images
Page 7: Ebet Roberts/Redferns
Page 8: ADEBARI/Stills/Gamma/Eyedea/Courtesy Everett Collection
Page 9: Ebet Roberts/Redferns
Page 10: David Sprague/WireImage
Page 11: Timothy A. Clary/AFP/Getty Images
Page 12: Steve Fenn ©ABC/Retna
Page 13: Mahesh Bhat/Getty Images
Page 14: Michael Ochs Archives/Getty Images
Page 16: © Tammie Arroy/AFF/Retna Ltd./Corbis
Page 17: Theodore Williams/Ebony Collection via AP Images
Page 18: Michael Ochs Archives/Getty Images
Page 19: Michael Ochs Archive/Getty Images
Page 20: Michael Ochs Archives/Getty Images
Page 21: CBS Photo Archive/Getty Images
Page 22: Michael Ochs Archives/Getty Images
Page 23: Gilles Petard/Redferns
Page 25: © Bettmann/Corbis
Page 26: Michael Ochs Archives/Getty Images
Page 27: Blank Archives/Getty Images
Page 28: Michael Ochs Archives/Getty Images
Page 30: Max B. Miller/Fotos International/Getty Images
Page 31: Michael Ochs Archives/Getty Images
Page 32: Michael Ochs Archive/Getty Images
Page 33: Michael Ochs Archives/Getty Images
Page 34: Michael Ochs Archives/Getty Images
Page 35, envelope: (cartoon still) Courtesy Everett Collection; (Jackson 5 ad) Courtesy *Cash Box* magazine, April 4, 1970
Page 35: Michael Ochs Archives/Getty Images
Page 36: Michael Ochs Archives/Getty Images
Page 37: Courtesy Deborah Dannelly
Page 38: CBS Photo Archive/Getty Images
Page 39: (top and bottom) Michael Ochs Archive/Getty Images
Page 40: (top and bottom) Courtesy Deborah Dannelly
Page 41: Michael Ochs Archives/Getty Images
Page 42: Michael Ochs Archives/Getty Images
Page 43: Michael Ochs Archives/Getty Images
Page 44: Michael Ochs Archives/Getty Images
Page 45: Fotos International/Getty Images
Page 46: Don Leavitt/Courtesy Everett Collection
Page 47: Michael Ochs Archives/Getty Images
Page 48: Jim McCrary/Redferns
Page 50: Tom Sheehan/Sony Music Archive/Getty Images
Page 51: CBS Photo Archive/Getty Images
Page 52: Richard E. Aaron/Redferns
Page 53: Ron Galella/WireImage
Page 54: Richard E. Aaron/Redferns
Page 55: Gregg Cobarr/WireImage
Page 56: Ebet Roberts/Redferns
Page 57: Mirrorpix/Courtesy Everett Collection
Page 58: © Universal Pictures/Courtesy Everett Collection
Page 59: AP Photo/George Brich
Page 60: (top) © Universal Pictures/Courtesy Everett Collection; (bottom) © Bettmann/Corbis
Page 61: Ebet Roberts/Redferns
Page 62: Ebet Roberts/Redferns
Page 63: Isaac Sutton/Ebony Collection via AP Images
Page 64: Andy Freeberg/Getty Images
Page 65: Michael Ochs Archive/Getty Images
Page 66: © Lynn Goldsmith/Corbis
Page 68: Ron Galella/WireImage
Page 69: (top) Chris Walter/WireImage; (bottom) Echoes/Redferns
Page 70: © Walter Mcbride/Retna Ltd./Corbis
Page 71: Courtesy Everett Collection
Page 72: (top) Ron Galella/WireImage; (bottom) © Bettmann/Corbis
Page 73: © Lynn Goldsmith/Corbis
Page 74: Courtesy Everett Collection
Page 75: © MCA/Universal/Courtesy Everett Collection
Page 76: Frank Edwards/Fotos International/Getty Images
Page 77, envelope: (press release) Courtesy CBS Entertainment
Page 77: © Wally McNamee/Corbis
Page 78: Ron Galella/WireImage
Page 79: Ron Galella/WireImage
Page 80: David McGough/DMI/Time & Life Pictures/Getty Images
Page 81: Michael Ochs Archives/Getty Images
Page 82: AP Photo/George Widman
Page 83: Michael Ochs Archives/Getty Images
Page 84: AP Photo/Mark Avery
Page 85: AP Photo/Lennox McLendon
Page 86: Chris Walter/WireImage
Page 87, envelope: (poster) artwork by J. Laramore
Page 87: AP Photo/Cliff Schiappa
Page 88: Michael Ochs Archives/Getty Images

Page 89: (top) Dave Hogan/Getty Images; (bottom) Dave Hogan/Hulton Archive/Getty Images
Page 90: GAB Archive/Redferns
Page 91: Jeffrey Mayer/WireImage
Page 92: Liaison
Page 94: © Buena Vista Pictures/Courtesy Everett Collection
Page 95: Dave Hogan/Getty Images
Page 96: Dave Hogan/Getty Images
Page 97: Bob Scott/Liaison
Page 98: John Chiasson/Liaison
Page 99: AP Photo/Gillian Allen
Page 100: © Duncan Raban/Stills/Retna Ltd./Corbis
Page 101: Kevin Mazur/WireImage
Page 102: AFP/Getty Images
Page 103, envelope: (newsletter) Courtesy Triumph International, Inc.; (shoe patent) United States Patent and Trademark Office
Page 103: Jean-Marc Giboux/Liaison
Page 104: Dave Hogan/Hulton Archive/Getty Images
Page 105: © Walter McBride/Retna Ltd./Corbis
Page 106: Kevin Mazur/WireImage
Page 107: © Stills/Retna Ltd./Corbis
Page 108: AFP/Getty Images
Page 109: (top) Hulton Archive/Getty Images; (bottom) Ron Galella/WireImage
Page 110: AP Photo/Mark Terrill
Page 111: Hulton Archive/Getty Images
Page 112: Gabriel Bouys/AFP/Getty Images
Page 113: Ron Galella/WireImage
Page 114: © Chris Good/Retna Ltd./Corbis
Page 115: Advertising Archive/Courtesy Everett Collection
Page 116: Phil Dent/Redferns
Page 118: L. Cohen/WireImage
Page 119: © HBO/Courtesy Everett Collection
Page 120: © David Lefranc/Kipa/Corbis
Page 121: Peter Still/Redferns
Page 122: Al Messerschmidt/NFL
Page 123, envelope: (mask) Artwork by Mark Ryden/Courtesy Deborah Dannelly
Page 123: Paul Bergen/Redferns
Page 124: Al Messerschmidt/Getty Images
Page 125: AP Photo/Douglas Pizac
Page 126: Ron Galella/WireImage
Page 127: James Mitchell/Ebony Collection via AP Images
Page 129: © Diego Goldberg/Corbis Sygma
Page 130: Courtesy Deborah Dannelly
Page 132: Mirrorpix/Courtesy Everett Collection
Page 130: Ron McMillan/Liaison
Page 134: PAT/ARNAL/Gamma/Eyedea/Courtesy Everett Collection
Page 135: Jeff Kravitz/FilmMagic
Page 136: Simon Ritter/Redferns
Page 138: Larry Busacca/WireImage
Page 139: Mirrorpix/Courtesy Everett Collection
Page 140: AP Photo
Page 141: (top) Photoshot/Courtesy Everett Collection; (bottom) Antonio Scorza/AFP/Getty Images
Page 142: Frank Micelotta/ImageDirect
Page 143: Mahesh Bhat/Getty Images
Page 144: Dave Hogan/Getty Images
Page 145: Dave Hogan/Getty Images
Page 146: Dave Hogan/Getty Images
Page 147: (top) Kieran Doherty/Redferns; (bottom) Rex USA/Courtesy Everett Collection
Page 148: Steve Fenn © ABC/Retna
Page 150: Courtesy Deborah Dannelly
Page 151: Kevin Mazur/WireImage
Page 152: Kevin Mazur/WireImage
Page 153: Eric Ryan/Getty Images
Page 154: David Sprague/WireImage
Page 155, envelope 9: (certificate) Courtesy Deborah Dannelly
Page 155: Tony Lewis/Newspix/Rex USA, Courtesy Everett Collection
Page 157: (top) Bill Robles/AFP/Getty Images; (bottom) Bob Covington/Getty Images
Page 158: Bob Galbraith-Pool/Getty Images
Page 159: Lora Schraft/AFP/Getty Images
Page 160: © Qi Heng/XinHua/Xinhua Press/Corbis
Page 162: WireImage
Page 163: © Kiyoshi Ota/Reuters/Corbis
Page 164: Tim Whitby/Getty Images
Page 165, envelope: (court document) Courtesy Everett Collection; (ticket) Courtesy Deborah Dannelly
Page 165: Dave Hogan/Getty Images
Page 166: Tim Whitby/Getty Images
Page 167: Simon James/Getty Images
Page 168: Sebastian Derungs/AFP/Getty Images
Page 169: Kevin Mazur/WireImage
Page 170: Stan Honda/AFP/Getty Images
Page 171: Julien Hekimian/WireImage
Page 172: Gabriel Bouys-Pool/Getty Images
Page 173: Dave Hogan/Getty Images
Page 174: Vivian Reed/VJR Photography
Page 176: Dave Hogan/Getty Images